D0557967

MODELS *of* PROFESSIONAL DEVELOPMENT

BRUCE JOYCE · EMILY CALHOUN

MODELS *of* PROFESSIONAL DEVELOPMENT

A Celebration *of* Educators

A JOINT PUBLICATION

CORWIN
A SAGE Company

For information:

Corwin
A SAGE Company
2455 Teller Road
Thousand Oaks, California 91320
(800) 233-9936
Fax: (800) 417-2466
www.corwin.com

SAGE India Pvt. Ltd.
B 1/I 1 Mohan Cooperative
   Industrial Area
Mathura Road, New Delhi 110 044
India

SAGE Ltd.
1 Oliver's Yard
55 City Road
London EC1Y 1SP
United Kingdom

SAGE Asia-Pacific Pte. Ltd.
33 Pekin Street #02-01
Far East Square
Singapore 048763

Printed in the United States of America.

Library of Congress Cataloging-in-Publication Data

Joyce, Bruce R.
Models of professional development: a celebration of educators / Bruce Joyce, Emily Calhoun.
A Joint Publication With the National Staff Development Council
     p. cm.
Includes bibliographical references and index.
ISBN 978-1-4129-7806-4 (pbk.)
    1. Teachers—In-service training. I. Calhoun, Emily. II. Title.

LB1731.J678 2010
370.71'55—dc22   2009043855

This book is printed on acid-free paper.

10 11 12 13 14 10 9 8 7 6 5 4 3 2 1

Acquisitions Editor:	Dan Alpert
Associate Editor:	Megan Bedell
Production Editor:	Libby Larson
Copy Editor:	Paula L. Fleming
Typesetter:	C&M Digitals (P) Ltd.
Proofreader:	Caryne Brown
Indexers:	Bruce Joyce & Emily Calhoun
Cover Designer:	Scott Van Atta (from a concept by Bruce Joyce and Ron Brandt)

Dedicated to

Edith Tayloe and Harlequin
The support system we love

Contents

provides a procedure for governing itself where 80 percent is the majority needed to make decisions and adopt initiatives.

Here some professionals are designated to provide help to others. In some ways this type of staff development has evolved from supervision, but some forms of coaching are new on the scene and have marked differences from the supervisory mode. Personal service can be open-ended or structured.

The school as an organization is on stage, with the development of teachers and principals into learning communities. These models also can be open-ended or take the form of disciplined action research.

Because many people are involved, formal, scheduled courses and workshops are prominent as are well-developed curriculums. Their content is ways of teaching.

No treatise on staff development would be complete without contemplating the currently both most criticized and most common way of organizing people for instruction of various sorts—the menus of brief workshops offered on days designated for staff training. As battered as it is, this mode can be made to be really effective, and professional development organizers should not dismiss it out of hand. Alternative ways of rescheduling already paid-for time generate new opportunities for this and other arrangements for staff development.

The nature of knowledge won through practice and the yield of knowledge from formal evaluations and research are considered here. There is little programmatic research at present, but the emperor does have some research clothes to go with practice-developed knowledge.

The field of professional development is ripe for careful evaluations, descriptive research, and studies of various practices.

Includes books, articles, and Web sites not cited in the body of the text but that can help the reader navigate the field of staff development.

Prologue

This book presents an inquiry into professional development aimed at sorting out its varieties, the organizational processes designed to make them work, and the effects they can have when they are implemented properly.

We have assembled information from four sources:

First is the set of commonly used models of professional development; we find them in practice and in books and articles describing and advocating them.

Second are sources of data about professional development and its organizational context. These take the form of reports of formal research, descriptions of action research and evaluation of particular approaches, and reports of practice. Studies of learning by educators and effects on student learning are a small but highly important source.

Third are studies of the intricate layers of the organizations in which staff development models are sheltered and where healthy nests need to be developed if any model is to succeed.

Fourth are reports of rarely used but promising models, ones we can project as feasible on a larger scale.

Altogether the results of our inquiry amount to a description of the current models of staff development, potential future ones, and a consideration of the organizational characteristics that need to be addressed to bring any of them to life.

The Strength of the Knowledge Base

Candidly, research on professional development is in its infancy, although formal research began to appear 30 years ago. However, the

1

field has not attracted programmatic researchers—those who pick up a model and conduct a series of studies to generate precise information about its effects and how to reshape it for greater effect. Related fields have yielded relevant information—for example, there is a large body of research on various models of teaching and teaching practices—but the important related fields of school improvement and organizational development have not attracted much programmatic research either.

Conducting research on staff development is technically demanding for several reasons, which we can illustrate by considering the evaluation of any particular approach or model:

> First, quality of implementation becomes a factor. A potentially effective model comes to life in the complex organization of schools and schooling and has to be of high quality if it is to be fairly evaluated. For example, during the development of professional learning communities in a large school district, the quality of the organizational climate of the schools can vary considerably. In some poor climates, the communities may not develop at all. In others, thriving communities may develop. The researcher has to contend with variance in implementation.

> Second, where effects on student learning are important, the effects on educators have to be studied first. And there is almost surely variance in what the educators learn and implement that has to be measured if effects on students are to be assessed.

> Third, a number of models of staff development are designed to help teachers alone, in groups, or in faculties to generate their own directions for growth. And those will not be identical. Essentially, the teachers and administrators will legitimately go in many directions. When that happens (and it should happen if the model does its job), the growth of neither teachers nor students can be specified and measured in advance.

> Fourth, the various models have somewhat different objectives— they are directed toward different aspects of educator behavior. Consequently, comparative studies are difficult. No single dependent variable (such as the use of a new teaching practice) covers the objectives of all the models.

These considerations and the relatively small amount of programmatic research combine to make general assessments of staff development very difficult. Those who hope to do a meta-analysis of the research literature and come up with a series of best options will be disappointed. But we are confident that many fine options for staff development exist. And there are enough data to allow us to be optimistic.

When we bring the scattered evidence together, we can conclude with confidence that teachers (and principals) have wonderful learning capacity and can learn from a variety of models. Far more important than a hunt for what model is most effective is a storehouse of models that can work well if properly implemented. Poor implementation can make any model ineffective. Conversely, a good learner does not make a poor approach effective.

Thus our contention that the critical question with respect to research on staff development is "What is good for what?" Because the likely outcomes from the various families of models can be significantly different, the big question is less "What works best?" than "What do I want to achieve?"

The knowledge base will get better. Efforts to survey the existing evaluations, studies, and relevant work from school renewal are increasing. For example, the recent effort for the National Staff Development Council by a team headed by Linda Darling-Hammond is particularly important for its breadth and because it should engender serious discussions about what is known and the kinds of studies that are badly needed (see Darling-Hammond, Wei, Andree, Richardson, & Orphanos, 2009).

Within the following chapters, we have included detailed descriptions of several studies where we have collaborated with school districts to evaluate intensive professional development programs and conduct research within them. These are included because they illustrate the complexity of embedded formative and summative studies. They all illustrate how the lines between evaluation and research become blurred as schools and school districts address their practical need to assess their efforts and have to explore theoretical issues when they innovate in staff development and school renewal.

What Makes a Model of Professional Development?

A model is a prototype, a pattern that, in education, can be used to create an environment for learning. Polished, a model takes on aspects of the ideal: at least a good way of doing things, though not the only way. As we looked at current and recommended practice, we selected as models approaches with the following characteristics:

First, they have a view of how people learn skills, acquire knowledge, and develop beliefs and attitudes. In the literature, the view is sometimes more implicit than explicit, but it is there.

Second, that view is connected to objectives—to particular skills, knowledge, and beliefs that are engendered by the model.

Third, the approach is clear, practical, and, therefore, disseminable.

Fourth, their implementation is measurable—we can document whether the aimed-for objectives are attained and to what degree.

Fifth, if the objectives for educators are believed to connect with student learning, the types of learning can be specified and measured.

These criteria make up the attributes of the types of professional development that we have netted from the literature and our knowledge of practice. As we will see, the models that emerged are not mutually exclusive. They are discernibly different, but they overlap and can even depend on parts of one another.

What makes a family of models? Throughout the book we will use these criteria as we describe families of models and the knowledge underpinning them. What is a family? It is simply a cluster of approaches to staff development that share specific attributes to a considerable extent. The members of a family are not identical, or they would have disappeared into one another, but they are more alike than different.

More about this later as we work through the models and families.

Terms

The language of professional development is not standardized. In these pages we use several terms that frequently have different meanings in various contexts and several different terms that have the same or similar meanings.

Let's begin with . . .

Inservice education, staff development, professional development, and professional learning. Until the early 1970s learning opportunities for educators were called "inservice education." For the most part, university courses were being referred to. Then, "staff development" was invented to refer not only to study in universities but also to opportunities developed and offered by school districts and states. Today, "professional development" is becoming more common, partly to embrace school-generated opportunities as well as the others. The term *development* bothers some, and we hear "professional learning" in some districts, but it does not have general acceptance. We are happy with both staff and professional development and slide from one to the other.

Repertoire. This term refers to the body of professional knowledge and skill possessed by a practitioner. It can also refer to the body of knowledge of a group of teachers or even a whole staff. The repertoire can range very widely. Some teachers (look at Nancy in Chapters 1 and 2) have many ways of teaching and can draw on them as appropriate. Some have a very limited repertoire. There are many implications for staff development. For example, if a mentor has a limited range but is paired with a mentee with a very large range . . . draw your own conclusions.

Training. Coming out of applied psychology, *training* refers to the conditions that are developed to help someone learn knowledge and skill in some domain of performance—both knowledge and skill are included as objectives. Training methods vary widely, from the nondirective to collective inquiry and to highly sequenced sets of learning activities. In education some believe that the term has negative connotations. We do not. It applies to the education of brain surgeons, rocket scientists, and the tutors of beginning readers. We see it as a generic term with no ideological connotations attached to it.

Recitation. The REALLY TRADITIONAL mode of teaching. Studies of teaching have confirmed what informal observation can ascertain—a pattern of teaching where students are exposed to some content or skill and then questioned about it. The teacher can assign material to be read and then quiz the students—recitation being their response. The research on teaching has indicated that many, probably most, teachers were "brought up" on recitation and that it is the main staple of their repertoire. The implications are important in the planning of staff development. If the providers' primary repertoire is recitation, then that is what their students (your teachers) are exposed to. If it is the primary repertoire of a mentor, then the mentee is pushed in that direction.

Implementation. Important is the distinction between the nominal adoption of a model and *really* doing it. We can see this where districts hire folks who are assigned to "coach" the faculties of schools but then have to go door-to-door to find teachers who would like to be exposed to their wares. Models come to life when they are implemented. That is, they have a good method, and they are connected with their clients interactively and with enough time to get the job done.

Solving the Time Problem: Something Everybody Has to Do to Ensure Success

In spite of the general agreement by professional educators, the public, and legislative bodies that the health and growth of teachers are basic to the health of schools, existing staff development is crammed into a tiny space of money and time. All approaches labor under these constraints and are hampered by them.

The contrast with some other occupational groups and professions is dramatic.

Let's consider the stories of Ted, Joe, and Amanda. None of them would identify themselves as professional educators. Ted is an accountant. Joe is a dentist. Amanda is a hairdresser. Ted (a practitioner of 40 years) and his primary staff in their firm in Menlo Park, California, attend a monthly one-day seminar and a yearly one- to two-week seminar on the practice of accounting and changes in regulations about taxes. Let's average this out at about 20 days a year. They pay for these seminars themselves, by the way, not to mention days the income lost when they could be selling services but are in study. Joe and his staff in Saint Simons Island, Georgia, study new techniques about 10 to 12 days per year. Amanda, also of Saint Simons Island, travels to Atlanta, Savannah, or Jacksonville for workshops that consume about 10 days per year, days in which she has no earnings but, rather, often pays for the service she receives. She also provides training in her specialties.

Ted, Joe, and Amanda are fine representatives of modern continuing education in their professions. They have good help, and they are not alone as they try to enhance their job-related knowledge and skills. Their occupational groups have tried to connect their practitioners to state-of the-art practice and trends. Lifelong occupational learning is routine for them.

Teaching is quite a different kettle of fish. *Formal staff development for the average practitioner is usually paid for by the organization—the school district*—but occupies only three or four days each year (see Cook, 1997, for a discussion of causes and remedies of the time problem).

And rather than seeking the same types of training as Ted, Joe, and Amanda do, teachers, administrators, and central office personnel express considerable dissatisfaction with the content and process of the workshops that are offered in those few days. For 20 years, authorities in the field have criticized the most common practices—the sets of brief workshops, and, by implication, the people who plan the smorgasbords of workshops—but the time allotment remains unchanged. What is so peculiar is that, in education, the employer pays for development opportunities for most practitioners but is often castigated for what it does, not for the small amount of time paid for but for how teachers, administrators, and central office personnel—the people who plan the workshops—feel about it and its effect on practice. For Ted, Joe, and Amanda, implementation is their responsibility (and all three work in view of colleagues and with them as they try to use new procedures in their workplaces), yet they continue regularly and actively to seek out more development, finding it of value.

A Nagging Thought

Is it possible that much of the perceived weakness in education staff development AND the din of criticism about it are products of its briefness? Would longer, stronger, workshops be both more effective and less criticized? Would a more collaborative workplace generate a more positive climate and greater satisfaction? We believe this is worth thinking about. In our own work where we have helped teachers learn more effective curriculums in the literacy area, the districts and schools have needed to expand greatly the amount of time available for study. In other words, the organizations have invested more heavily in the education of their faculties. How long will that investment be continued? Some of our client-partners have continued to dig down for as much as ten years, but some, generally because a new superintendent is not oriented toward staff development, wind down gradually. We need to spread the word that investment in people is a core, essential expense that strengthens competence and professionalism, builds morale, and lets imaginations soar as we improve and ultimately re-create education.

1

The Faces of Professional Development in Education

Multiple Intelligences at Work

I'd like to find a one best way, but that's just not the way it is.

—our reflective observer

Organizations—Models—Environments—Professional Growth

Forty years ago Bob Schaefer (1967) had it right in *The School as a Center of Inquiry.* He portrayed the school as a place where both students and educators are inquirers, where attention to learning by teachers and administrators has a place side by side with learning by students.

Schools are designed to teach students how to learn. Primarily, this is accomplished by healthy and growing educators. Our best and most exciting schools are places where the adult educators are in a high state of growth and give each other energy, knowledge, and skill. A high-growth environment for the adults infects the students.

Staff development is about learning—the belief that we are never finished. Our need for learning does not put us down but rather opens a better quality of professional and personal life. Also, students learn in proportion to the amount of learning that we do. Our learning propels their learning.

Professional development comes into being through deliberate actions by the organization—usually the district or school, sometimes the state or province—to generate learning by educators, to make the school a learning laboratory for teachers and administrators. These actions result in the various forms of staff development that are practiced today. These forms are directed toward several purposes, including

- Enhancing the school as a good place for learning by educators
- Enhancing the school as an organization, one that generates a high quality of life for students and staff alike
- Providing opportunities for professional learning by staff, from basic knowledge and skill to new approaches to curriculum and instruction, including tools for inquiring into student learning
- Enhancing the collaborative dimension of the school and reducing isolation, enabling the faculty to work together to help the students reach high states of growth

Note that several of these purposes deal simultaneously with improving the organizational climate of schools and the states of growth of the educators. Helping educators have a better quality of experience in the workplace and helping the school become a more positive and warm institution are worthwhile in themselves. These become the focus of the first level of evaluation in staff development and school renewal. Also, a generative social climate will lead to efforts to better curriculum and instruction for students, but as a derivative of educators' growth. However, in the models where curricular and instructional initiatives are central, the growth of the educators needs to lead directly to increased student learning.

Importantly, an approach to professional development can legitimately be used before there is solid evidence that student learning will change or increase. In fact, the most common forms of professional development do not have clear evidence of the student learning that will come from them. In the future, the evaluation of all approaches needs to generate documented educator learning, and the evaluation of initiatives in curriculum and instruction needs always to include the study of student learning.

Now, let's look at the most common ways that professional development services are provided to educators. Then, let's look at the processes by which they are nested in school and state organizations.

Variations on a Professional Development Theme

We imposed a definition of *staff/professional development* as formal provisions by organizations of ways of helping teachers and administrators develop a better workplace and enhance their knowledge and competence in their assigned roles. *Formal*, as used here, means the deliberate arrangement of organizational processes and structures to facilitate the development of competence of teachers and school-level administrators. Clearly, there are myriad ways that four million-plus teachers and administrators can generate growth opportunities on their own. However, our central focus here is on the opportunities for learning that are purposely created by states, districts, or schools (the organizational entities of the educational system), including the creation of opportunities for individual educators and small groups to generate initiatives. (The formal can generate the informal.)

Varieties of Current and Common Practice in Staff Development: A List in Random Order

To get going, let's think about the following ways that education organizations generate learning opportunities for their personnel.

- *Individual inquiry*—Individuals are supported with time and money in their personal study efforts. Stipends (grants) and brief leaves offer opportunities. Teachers apply for the opportunity. In some rare but interesting cases, modest resources are made available to all teachers. Bruce is currently consulting in a pair of schools where $2,000 is set aside each year for learning projects by each of the teachers. That is a rare practice, but exemplary.
- *Personal/professional services by peers*—Teachers disseminate instructional improvement, usually to novices but to other experienced teachers as well. Mentoring programs directed at new teachers is a prominent example. In recent years, there has been a marked increase of services both for broad areas of teaching and for specific curriculum areas. These are usually called "coaching" programs, as in the much-promoted practice of connecting literacy coaches to schools. Nationally, about 6,000 coaches were supported by No Child Left Behind (Reading First) resources last year. The National Council of Teachers of English is lobbying for 10,000 "literacy coaches" (see Hall, 2004).
- *Personal/professional services by supervisors*—For many years, school districts emphasized structured instructional improvement

through supervision, where ideas about instruction are disseminated by supervisors, including principals (seen as instructional leaders). Over the last 50 years, districts have probably invested more resources in supervision than any other form of staff development. Supervision began when the typical school reached the size where it had a full-time principal (although teaching principals had supervisory duties as well). In addition to adding principals, districts added full-time supervisory personnel to their central offices, as well as coordinators in the core curriculum areas.

  o Some mentoring and coaching programs utilize procedures (as in the "preconference–observation–postconference" pattern) adopted directly from supervision (see, especially, the work of Madeline Hunter, 1980, which dominated staff development for 20 years, and Goldhammer, Anderson, & Krajewski, 1980, on clinical supervision). Today collegial interchange is emphasized, and there is greater equality in relationships, at least on the surface.

- *Action research*—This is disciplined inquiry by faculties who study curriculum, instruction, and the social climate of their schools and make decisions about school improvement initiatives. An inquiry paradigm is followed, leading staffs to study student learning, local community conditions, and the literature in one or more of the core curriculum areas. Action research can result from open-ended learning community activity or begin with the formal introduction of the inquiry paradigm. Action research itself has been a long line of inquiry, including luminaries from Lewin, Corey, and Deming to the present scholars of the process (see Emily's *Action Research in the Self-Renewing School* [Calhoun, 1994]).

- *Open-ended local learning community activity*—School-based teams come together to assess their situation and make decisions about needed improvements. In some districts, all teachers are members of learning community teams. In others, the practice is voluntary. In some, the whole staff is organized as a single learning community (see Schmoker, 2004).

- *Curriculum and instructional initiatives*—These are usually focused on one or another of the core curriculum areas. Again, there are many current examples in the literacy area, as fresh curriculums and models of teaching are developed and disseminated. Initiatives of this sort are complex and require considerable effort throughout the organization (see Joyce & Showers, 2002; Joyce, Weil, & Calhoun, 2009).

- *Workshops on generic instructional techniques*—Examples are types of questioning, classroom management devices, simple cooperative strategies, and the like (see Marzano, 2003). These make up a fairly large portion of the menus of workshops offered on "staff development days." They are directly relevant to practice but are less powerful than either full-blown models of teaching or curriculums in the core subject areas (see Joyce et al., 2009).

- *Sets of workshops scheduled during paid "staff development days"*—The core purpose here is to bring people together for study. Essentially, arrangements are made for menus of workshops on various topics presented on a small number of days each year when teachers and principals are paid to participate. Currently, these are heavily criticized by national organizations.

Distance learning is an approach not quite parallel to those above. It is on the rise, with online courses and a host of workshops mediated by e-books, DVDs, and streaming. Distance learning technologies might spawn a variety of innovative forms of professional development and just might ignite a wide-reaching revolution in the field. PBS has recently pulled together an enormous library of interviews, videos of scenes, and so on that represent this emerging revolution.

What Do We Have Here?

The approaches described just above are different from one another but are not completely so. Their processes and purposes overlap, and what begins in one area can generate an event or program in another. Some, like the designated professional day workshops and courses and workshops on generic teaching methods, are centered on the formal delivery of services, but they can include many modes of instruction. Direct personal service can generate curriculum implementation. When curriculums and models of teaching are developed and disseminated, learning communities can be developed.

Families of Models

We have collapsed the approaches into several categories, or families, of models that will form much of the structure of the book.

Supporting the Individual

Although all of staff development intends to support individuals, some types focus on the individual as a person and provide avenues for people to grow according to their own lights. Vastly underused, this family has tremendous promise.

$_\nu$ Personal/Professional Service

Here, some teachers and administrators are designated to provide help to others. In some ways, this type of staff development has evolved from supervision, but some forms of coaching are new on the scene and are markedly different from the supervisory mode. Personal service can be either open-ended or structured.

Social Construction of Knowledge and Action

The school as an organization is on stage, with the development of learning communities. This family can be very open-ended or take the form of disciplined action research.

Curricular/Instructional Initiatives

The course and workshop are prominent; developed ways of teaching or the dissemination of curriculums are the content of formal workshops and courses.

The Infamous Menus of Brief Workshops

No treatise on staff development would be complete without contemplation of the currently most criticized and most common way of organizing people for study—the menus of brief workshops on designated staff development days. Despite the critiques, when properly executed, this mode can be effective, and staff development organizers should not dismiss it out of hand.

In all our categories, inquiry and self-development are central to high-quality programs. Also, emerging media can carry many kinds of content—distance education can instigate and support processes as well.

We need to start by thinking about the processes that give any of these families—in fact any good idea—a niche within the organization.

Organizational/Implementation Layers: Making Nests Within the Cultural System

Staff development models take place in organizations. A number of organizational processes have to be engaged in if an idea is to become an active practice. The following set of processes is probably a minimum.

As we introduce them, we will illustrate how they apply when an individual generates a personal program of study, a small group engages in an inquiry, and a district of some size begins the study of a curriculum area.

Three Parallel Examples

At the individual level, we are thinking of a woman we will call Nancy. Nancy is trying to learn how to assess her sixth-grade students' writing more effectively. She has read about a system for studying quality of writing, has looked at a copy of the manual, and has decided that she would like to go to a three-day workshop to examine it more closely and work with others who are trying to learn to use it. She needs some resources and will have to communicate those needs to folks who hold some of the purse strings.

Even when a small group develops a plan, a surprising amount of decision making is involved about not only what to do but who will carry out essential tasks. As we write this, we are thinking of a small group of teachers from one school (let's call them the Synergy Team) who are planning to go to the annual conference of a national organization in their field. Primarily they want to study procedures for increasing reading and writing vocabulary, the focus of a two-day preconference session and several special sessions during the four day conference. Right now they have realized that their group comprises the entire primary faculty of that school. Providing substitutes for a week will be costly *and* entail ensuring that the substitute teachers are both competent and well-prepped. They also did not expect that parents might raise objections, but some are doing so. A public relations effort has to be organized *posthaste*.

Let's also think about the superintendent of a 50-school district and his chief planners, whom we will call the School Improvement Group (SIG). The literacy curriculum has been on the front of their plate for some time. They have made a decision to begin by increasing the capacity of the school staffs to assess student learning in reading. Next, they need to examine measurement instruments, decide how to begin, and start communicating their intentions to the considerable number of teachers and administrators who form their faculties.

Creating an Action Plan

Creating an action plan is not analogous to planning the Battle of Normandy. That said, however, the steps to getting things going have to be spelled out in sufficient detail that implementation is possible.

Nancy has the easiest time making her action plan because she does not intend to involve anyone else. She knows she wants to explore the scale for studying writing and doesn't need to make further plans until she decides how well it works.

Our Synergy Team has to plan travel, conference registration, accommodations, tickets to special events, and so on. They also have to find and prepare substitutes and plan events to communicate what they are doing to parents, not to mention possibly nervous administrators. Further, the group will need to get together when they get back, evaluate what they have learned, and prepare to practice and implement the strategies they find useful. That means restructuring time considerably

The District SIG group needs to identify potential instruments and make decisions about whether to select the same instrument to use throughout the district or present a set of instruments to the school faculties for their deliberation. They decide to select the Gunning (1998) procedures in their K–1 classes and the Gray Oral Reading Test (Wiederholt & Bryant, 2001) in the Grade 2 to 6 classrooms. They will have to communicate the basis for their selections to school personnel. And they will need to prepare a good-sized team to administer the tests and interpret the results from all schools. The SIG group decides to organize an assessment cadre made up of two teachers from each school and a number of central office personnel. The superintendent decides that he and his chief deputies and all SIG members will be part of the cadre.

Assembling Adequate Resources and Arrangements

The action plan generates needs for human and monetary resources. A school faculty that wants to add a technology or teaching model to its repertoire may have to find and pay a consultant. They may have to find time for teachers to plan and debrief together.

Nancy has to approach her principal and, more than likely, a district committee. Her budget for the three-day conference, including airfare, hotel, meals, and tuition, is about $2,000. Two days for a substitute teacher are additional. Her district doesn't have the formal provisions for individual stipends and short leaves that we describe and recommend in Chapter 2. So she has to ask for what amounts to a grant from the district. Because she works with many children from low socioeconomic status (SES) households, the district can tap into its Title I funds for school renewal and does so. If she worked largely with children from middle-class families, finding money for her would be much more complicated.

Our Synergy Team scrounges for travel money: airfare, accommodations, food. They can make all necessary arrangements themselves but might use a travel agent to help find best fares and such.

The District SIG group has a complex job, but its members are close to the policy-making apparatus. Finding experts to help them will take energy, study, and know-how.

Implementation: Putting the Plan Into Action and Activating the Resources

This is where the rubber meets the road. And implementation is vital. Implementation bridges the planning and budgeting process to create the envisioned actions. Worthwhile goals require real changes.

Nancy has the simplest job. At one of her regular meetings with the parents of her students, she explains what she wants to do: try out the new scale with her students and network with teachers in other schools, mostly in other states, whom she will meet at the conference. She will use e-mail, fax, and telephone.

Our Synergy Team will probably find that communication with the parents is one of its trickiest tasks. Meetings and personal conferences need to be planned. Second, getting together to consolidate what is learned will be more complicated than usual. Teachers in the primary grades have very little discretionary time. Classes may have to be "covered" to create time when they can all get together.

The SIG has a daunting task. Just organizing a cadre and providing adequate training are demanding. And as data are collected, the results have to be intelligibly communicated to the staffs of all the schools.

Formative Evaluation and Revision of Procedures

Most planned activities of any length and complexity need to be improved during implementation. Many promising staff development programs have had flaws that have been repeated year after year because procedures for taking stock and fixing problems with the initiative have not been in place. Let's not make that mistake!

Again, Nancy just does it. She examines the information she gets from the new scale, discussing her reactions with her new e-mail colleagues and the folks who conducted the workshops.

The Synergy Team needs to focus on making progress toward arrangements to get together and follow up on the conference experience. That, we believe, will be their most difficult task, one requiring close monitoring. Their first attempts to schedule times to meet may or may not work out well.

The District SIG will need to track the effects of the professional development offerings that will prepare its large cadre to make accurate assessments of the students' capacity to read. If reliability is not established, further training will have to be provided.

Periodic Summative Evaluation

Implementation takes first place in the evaluation scheme. We need to estimate when a good level of implementation can reasonably be expected to have been achieved. Then, we need to verify whether that level has been achieved.

Effects on Student Learning Is Next

Estimates are needed of when implementation could reasonably affect aspects of student learning. (Evaluating too soon is useless.) When effects can be reasonably expected, then assessments should be made to develop a picture of whether student achievement occurred as a consequence of implementation.

Nancy decides to use the scale in the next academic year to determine the effects of a new model of teaching she will be implementing.

Our Synergy Team needs to look carefully at the implementation of the conditions enabling follow-up on the conference experience. And they need to examine the product of their experience—asking whether they are better able to think about vocabulary development in their students and whether their teaching practice needs to change in any way. At that point, they may enter a new phase of decision making, determining whether to embark on a stage of studying curricular and instructional strategies in the vocabulary area.

The District SIG, beginning with the development of an assessment cadre, is positioning itself very well to examine student learning. However, no intervention is planned, and the planners can't select an intervention until they develop a reliable picture of the state of achievement in reading in their schools.

Not all organization development specialists would describe these processes in these terms, and some would believe that the sequence, as presented, is too linear. The important thing is the recognition that staff development initiatives, large and small, take place as organizational activity. You don't make significant changes without dealing *very* seriously with the organizational necessities (see Schmuck & Runkel, 1985; Seashore-Lewis & Miles, 1990).

Interactions Between Varieties of Professional Development and Organizational Processes

By now, you are surely thinking about how easily an initiative can slip through the organizational cracks. You can devise a promising initiative that seems to fit the bill of needs in the school or district. You find support for that variety in studies—research or well-designed evaluations—and in credible clinical experience. Then you begin to work your way through the organizational process layers. Too great a degree of failure in any one of them can stymie the actualization of a fine idea.

Note that you have the same types of technical and organizational problems whether you are planning to make an initiative centered on teacher learning communities or, like our SIG, you are charged with making a sweeping assessment and reflecting on whether the area (in their case, reading) needs serious intervention.

Goals and Organization of the Book

Our goals are to locate transportable models of staff development and find ways of making the varieties strong and successful.

Order of Presentation

We begin with the models that support the educator as an individual, because the central clients of professional development are the people who staff the schools and who, for the most part, are asked, as individuals, to carry out their duties. Beginning there also enables us to consider the characteristics of educators as learners and the kinds of organizational cultures that enable them to thrive. Next, we look at the models where individuals are asked to give service to other individuals in mentoring and coaching assignments. Third, we look at the models that are centered on collaboration as members of faculties and groups within faculties. The collaborative process becomes prominent, along with ways of conducting inquiries into teaching and learning and how to make them better. Fourth, we examine initiatives in curriculum and instruction that can be focused on schools or districts, small and large, and even states. Finally, we inquire into how to improve one of the most common and most criticized organizations of professional development—the menus that are offered on designated days or parts of days to the personnel of the school districts who organize them.

Thus, we move the focus from individuals to pairs, then to groups and school staffs, and thence to districts and states. Initiatives at all these levels can succeed. The richness of the array of models and the fine capacity of teachers combine to produce our optimistic state.

2

Supporting the
Individual Educator

Helping People Do Their Thing

I like working with others, but there are things I learn best when I'm just following my own nose.

—our reflective observer

We begin our report with a focus on the educator as an individual. We start here partly because teachers and principals are the central clients of professional development. In schools, most instruction is given by teachers working by themselves (in some cases paraprofessionals or teaching assistants are present). A goodly portion of staff development should be directed to these special individuals, who have a very personal responsibility for educating our children. And most of professional development for principals needs to focus on supporting and leading those teachers. All the other families of models will ultimately serve individuals but are organized through or toward groups of school and district staffs.

In this chapter we concentrate on five ways of generating individual growth. Two of these are concrete methods of direct support for personal inquiry:

  1. Offering stipends to help educators generate and capitalize on growth opportunities for themselves

  2. Offering short-term leaves for individual professional development

Together these prove a direct and powerful tool for directing energy toward growth. And they enhance professionalism as such. Knowing you are in charge of thinking about your knowledge and skills and taking steps to augment them generate a sense of personal expertness and pride.

Frequently individual inquiry will lead to learning to use new teaching skills and curriculum content, leading to

  3. Providing support as new knowledge and skills are implemented in the classroom and school

Implementation challenges us to redevelop content as we incorporate it into the process of teaching. We climb from the level of learning that we can obtain in the course or workshop and develop control over it as we incorporate it into our current practice. Here we need the support of others.

As distance staff development increases, this kind of support will be critical if the promise of new content is to be realized in practice.

Next we examine a model for using the organizational climate to help individuals develop, in turn, an affirmative climate for students, parents, and community.

  4. Building an energizing and positive culture in the district and school

This approach resides in the dimension of leadership that generates the social system of the school district and the schools. As we will see below, there is evidence that a substantial portion of outstanding student achievement is associated with elevating beliefs and actions. The effect is sufficient to bring achievement by low socioeconomic status (SES) students to levels equal to or above the levels of higher SES populations. Finally, we will discuss

  5. Using systems for studying teaching to help teachers analyze teaching and make decisions about enhancing their repertoire and doing so

This practice was common a number of years ago but has fallen into disuse, probably because the current generation of educational leaders and teachers was not taught how to do it.

Before we discuss these more fully, we need to consider several parts of the knowledge base that can help us fashion the models that serve individuals directly.

Critical Issues and Considerations

Because individual differences will strongly affect each of these approaches, we begin by looking at teachers as growing, continuously developing people and how personality affects capacity to learn new ways of teaching and new curriculums. Then we will examine studies that help us understand the social climate of districts and schools and how it influences the behavior of professionals, community members, parents, and students. And, then, we will examine a study in a school district where teachers responded to initiatives that provided them with stipends and short leaves, where they were faculty members in schools in which schoolwide action research was conducted, and where a major districtwide initiative in literacy was conducted. Finally, we will briefly consider studies where teachers learned to use curricular and instructional models, studies that provide evidence about the learning capacity of educators.

We will use the yield from these discussions of issues and considerations as we try to maximize both this family of professional development models and the other families that follow. In this discussion, we will try to provide information that is relevant to several questions:

- How do individual differences affect personal professional development and initiatives designed to support it? States of growth and conceptual complexity are considered.
- How does the culture of the school and district affect individuals? We will look at the cultures of high- and low-achieving schools serving communities that differ in socioeconomic character.
- How do individuals respond to initiatives providing them with resources to organize their own professional development activities?
- What have studies of school renewal initiatives taught us about the capability of teachers to teach themselves?

States of Growth and Personal/Professional Lives

That differences among people are important is not just a cliché. And the importance does not end with children. Everyone who teaches or has parented more than one child is keenly aware of commonality and distinctiveness. And both common characteristics and uniqueness enlarge as we emerge into adulthood. Over the last 30 years, we and our colleagues have conducted sets of studies on the relative "states of growth" of educators and the quality of their personal and professional lives. *States of growth* refers to the interaction of people with their environments from the perspective of how they use their environments as sources of support and development. In a certain sense, we all need to make use of our social and physical environments to survive and to thrive. In contrast with frames of reference that are focused on the quality of environments surrounding people and supporting them, we concentrate here how individuals draw sustenance from their situations. The people who do this best actually improve their milieus—they draw positive energy toward themselves. And they seek better and better circumstances from which they can grow—and to which they give. As we have studied teachers and other educators, we have discovered considerable similarities in how they behaved in personal and professional contexts. Here are the categories we arrived at as we summarized our findings (see Joyce, Weil, & Calhoun, 2009):

- *Gourmet omnivores*—These proactive, discriminating people generate opportunities for development for themselves and, often, for their consorts and close friends. They do a good job of drawing information from their environments and integrating it into their conceptual systems. Their conceptual levels (see below) tend to be high, and they exploit a variety of sources as they interact with their social milieu. In our various studies, a range of 10–15 percent of educators have been in this category. Their energy makes them natural leaders, although not all are gregarious or seek to lead.
- *Active consumers*—These people also seek experiences and exploit them. In a cohort with gourmet omnivores they behave very much like the gourmet omnivores, and they have high integrative complexity. They are less proactive than the gourmet omnivores and protect their opportunities for growth less militantly. About 20 percent of the people we have studied have been active consumers.
- *Passive consumers*—Our largest category by far, making up more than half of our populations. These people are dependent on their professional and social environments for stimulation and opportunities to grow. Thus, they move toward the more

active states summarized above when they are in the company of omnivores and active consumers and in situations rich with possibilities.

On the other hand, a group made up of passive consumers may fail to exploit even very rich environments unless it has stimulating leadership.

- *Reticent consumers*—Only about 5 to 10 percent of educators. These folks actually push away opportunities for growth and can actively discourage others. However, many leaders overestimate the number of persons in this stage. Educators, and middle-class people in general, do not like conflict, and resistors create the appearance of conflict, even when they express themselves only through grumbling. The similarities in professional and personal behavior are striking. They have a tendency to blame their environments—the rest of the school depresses them professionally; their neighborhood and home depress them personally.

To make any model of staff development work, we need to acknowledge both similarities and differences and modulate our initiatives to accommodate and take advantage of the differences. And a model that seems to work for some may not work for all unless there is modification for educators as people. Passive consumers may not express their needs well, so helping them do so is important. Reticent consumers are generally disliked by leaders, which doesn't help— they teach as many children as do the happiest campers. And the most active people can be neglected because a natural tendency is to assume that they will take care of themselves. As we will see when we discuss how to make brief workshops productive, workshops directed at the majority may not support the omnivores and active consumers.

We have been continually impressed by just how similarly individuals behave in their personal and professional lives. The gourmet omnivores exploit both personal and professional settings and enrich them as well. Passive consumers depend greatly on the company they keep, at home and in the office. The reticent folks are not impressed but stand aside, armed with cynical comments, in their homes, communities, and workplaces. Partly this is because different states of growth are generated by differences in personality, particularly how people process information.

Levels of states of growth are correlated with levels of conceptual complexity. In a long series of studies with our colleague David Hunt of the Ontario Institute for Studies in Education, we have examined the influence of conceptual complexity on teaching styles and on the acquisition of new curricular/instructional models. *Conceptual level* refers to the type of structures one brings to the environment. Simply put, the more simple and rigid the structure, the more likely it is that a person will accept information that supports the existing structure and reject contradictory information. The more complex the structure, the more places one has to examine information of all types and integrate it or, even, generate new structures to accommodate new ideas.

We can see conceptual level in teaching where, the greater the complexity of the teacher's information processing system,

- the more integrative the learning environment,
- the more that inductive inquiry is a part of the process of teaching,
- and the greater degree of acceptance of diverse student personalities. (For summaries, see Joyce & Showers, 2002, and Joyce et al., 2009).

In addition, the higher the conceptual level, the easier it is to learn and implement complex curricular/instructional models.

We are inclined to concentrate on the lighting of candles rather than the cursing of darkness and take the position that persons of all states of growth deserve support. Leaders should make considerable efforts to reach persons who come with different habits and help reticent and passive consumers to reach higher levels of development.

High- and Low-Achieving Schools— Culture and Professional Development

Two studies examined staff development in exceptionally high- and low-achieving schools in the state of Georgia, including the ethos in the districts where those schools operate. The studies were possible because through the 1990s, the state maintained a thorough database on student learning. The researchers selected 20 elementary, 20 middle, and 20 high schools, half of which had exceptionally high achievement for three years running and half of which had very low achievement for the same three years. For example, in the upper SES bracket of elementary schools, 91 percent of the students in the high-achieving schools reached the state goals on the tests compared to

61 percent of the students in the lower-achieving upper SES bracket. In two schools matched for size in the lower SES bracket, the top school was in the highest 20 percent for all schools in the state, and the lower school was in the bottom 20 percent for all schools in its SES cluster.

A team of researchers visited the schools and conducted interviews with teachers, principals, and district officials. The interviewers were unaware of the achievement status of the schools.

The schools had roughly equal monetary resources for staff development, including for released time, and had similar pools of district and regional providers of staff development to draw on. Differences could be seen in how professional development and school improvement initiatives were governed, the kinds of staff development processes that were used, and the relationship between district leadership and school personnel.

In the higher-achieving schools, governance was broader and more integrative—decision making was shared, and communication was thorough.

The objectives of the resulting staff development were clearly to make productive changes in curriculum and instruction—ones that would increase student learning. Workshops employed more complex processes, and teachers and principals were organized to work together to implement the content of the training. And teachers and administrators reported that good levels of implementation did take place.

Interestingly, in the higher-achieving schools, the district administrators both pushed and pulled more. Simultaneously they broadened decision making and strongly encouraged positive change. They blended top-down and bottom-up behaviors (Harkreader & Weathersby, 1998).

The Iowa School Boards Association built on the Georgia database and conducted ethnographic analyses of a set of school districts selected because they housed some of the exceptionally high- and low-achieving schools identified by Harkreader and Weathersby (1998). The Iowa team studied the views of the superintendents, board members, district and school administrators, and teachers. They concluded that certain beliefs about students and parents pervaded the ethos of the districts. In high-achieving schools, the attitude toward students and parents was positive and optimistic—the term *elevating* was coined. Both education professionals and lay board members felt that students could learn and could be taught to learn more effectively. In the districts housing the low-achieving schools, the view was negative and hopeless. Laypeople and professionals "accepted" the position that the students were limited and came from limited homes. Only low levels of achievement could be expected (Iowa Association of School Boards, 2007).

From these studies it appears that staff development was conducted less mechanistically and more integratively in the high-achieving schools and that the ethos of the school district was different in those districts that contained the high- and low-achieving schools. Also, differences in SES did not explain differences in achievement or ethos. Rather, in that state, some of the highest-achieving schools were in the lower SES categories, and some of the lowest-achieving schools were in the higher SES categories. School and district culture trumped SES.

> *Message*—Building an affirmative ethos enhances the quality of professionalism and the nature of professional development. Essentially, an important way to support teachers is to lead the district and school toward a positive social climate—an elevating culture.

Now, let's look at a study that compared three modes of governance of staff development: governance by individuals, by school faculties, and by the entire district in the form of curricular/instructional initiatives in literacy, specifically in writing.

Initiatives by Individuals, Schools, and District: Are There Differences?

As we indicated earlier, many current writers about staff development are supportive of governance styles where teachers design their staff development or have considerable influence on content and design ("bottom-up" modes). Those writers are wary of designs made by local or state officials ("top-down" modes). As far as we know, only one study made a direct comparison of governance modes, and we were principals in the study and publication of the results. The findings were interesting.

The study was possible because all the elementary school teachers experienced staff development from three governance modes simultaneously over a two-year period. One was a districtwide initiative in the language arts. Teachers were involved in the selection and conduct of the initiative, but it was implemented across the district, and staff development was provided to all teachers on a regular basis.

The second was schoolwide action research. Each school was provided with a budget for self-study, and leadership teams made up of principals and teachers were responsible for leading the effort, which was to involve all the teachers at each school. Third was the support of teachers as individuals with stipends that they could use to further their personal study. However, the support of the teachers as individuals had considerable effects—a great many individual projects were generated (Joyce, Calhoun, Carran, Simser, Rust, & Halliburton, 1996). The effort has positive messages for the support of individuals.

The teachers described their estimates of the effects of the three initiatives. Nearly everybody was positive toward his or her experiences with all of them, and all believed that each had made important changes and enhanced student learning. However, a third of the teachers did not generate individual projects, whereas all were involved in the school- and districtwide processes.

As to objectives, the individuals were free to develop their own, as were the schools. The district initiative focused on improving quality of writing.

The entire effort affected student learning considerably. Measures of quality of writing indicated considerable improvement in quality of writing—the average student gained about twice as much during a year as had been the norm in previous years. Fourth-grade students ended the first year above where eighth-grade students had begun the year.

We wish that there were more studies of governance, particularly because the literature makes so much of locus of control, and the assumption is often made that control needs to be at the school, teaching team, or even grade-level unit. The real issue may be in how to make the several types of governance pay off for various purposes. Possibly, governance structures for districtwide initiatives may be quite different from structures to support teachers as individuals, and those may be different from the structures that support school-based efforts effectively.

Messages About Teachers From Studies of Change in Curriculum and Instruction

Studies of curriculum implementation offer a test of not only the types of staff development that focuses on curriculum implementation—see Chapters 5, 6, and 7—but of teacher learning capacity as well. The question of whether teachers can master new curricular patterns has been dealt with on a very large scale by the developers and evalua-tors of Success for All (Slavin & Madden, 2001) and Reading Recovery (Swartz & Klein, 1997). In both cases, thousands of teachers have been able to implement curriculums involving new practices, and consid-erable numbers of students have learned to read better as a result.

Some extraordinary findings from long-ago studies in preservice teacher education and staff development have been virtually for-gotten in recent years. Thirty years ago a series of studies on "microteaching," and "minicourses" focused on training. Teachers practiced instructional skills they were exposed to through demon-stration videotapes and print material and gave themselves feedback by videotaping themselves and comparing their performance to videotaped prototypes. The minicourses covered more than 20 com-plex teaching skills. A very important result was the addition of infor-mation about how well teachers can teach themselves, provided that the theory-demonstration-practice paradigm (again, see Chapter 5) was followed during training (Borg, Langer, & Gall, 1970). These programmatic research efforts generated those two very important conclusions—that teachers could learn a considerable variety of teaching skills *and* that they could do so when studying alone. The caveat here is that the minicourse program provided a great deal of material, including demonstrations, and the means by which the teachers could match their behavior to the depictions of skill in those demonstrations.

The findings from these studies that give us information about the capacity of teachers to learn new teaching strategies and curriculums are all positive. Although alternative sets of training elements and "follow-up" will probably be developed, current knowledge indi-cates that nearly all teachers can expand their repertoires and, pro-vided the new repertoires will generate new types or degrees of student learning, achieve the level of implementation where students will benefit.

The Menu of Promising Models to Serve Individuals

Because direct support for individuals has been so meager, our mod-els for individual support are more possibilities than reality, but the possibilities are fascinating. We will elaborate on the ones listed at the beginning of the chapter. Others can also be developed, but these make a beginning in this remarkably underorganized area.

Concrete methods of direct support for personal inquiry include two that can work together.

1. Offering stipends to help educators generate and capitalize on growth opportunities for themselves
2. Offering short-term leaves for individual professional development

The Joyce, Calhoun, Carran, Simser, Rust, and Halliburton (1996) studies helped us understand the implications of the very real individual differences in response to initiatives.

For several years all teachers in the district were offered stipends for their own self-education projects. In the peak year, these amounted to $1,000.

A short plan was required, but very few plans were turned down. Teachers attended a large variety of workshops, courses, and conferences, and one art teacher added some of his own money and went to the Yucatan to develop a unit on pre-Columbian art.

From our perspective, the program provided excellent support, leading to a variety of self-selected self-education projects. The teachers who participated were uniformly positive about this type of support. However, we learned that there were considerable individual differences in response. In fact, one-third of the teachers did not take advantage of the opportunity. That third did not apply for the funds. That they didn't participate does not indicate that the program was a failure. Rather, it underlined that individual differences *do* exist. Two-thirds of the teachers made good use of the opportunity. One third did not. We advocate this type of support but need to caution that even something that seems so exciting will not reach everyone. Not to worry—no form of support will do so. And some people need more support than others to maximize participation in many of the models we are discussing. Passive consumers appear to profit more when they are in the company of active consumers and gourmet omnivores.

Short-term leaves make a lot of sense. A small number of districts offer short-term leaves so that teachers can engage in studying and finding and developing curriculum materials. A wealth of areas can be studied, and many teachers can seek enrichment if they can have a two- or three-week period to take advantage of the goods that are there for the picking in many areas.

Frequently individual inquiry will lead to learning to use new teaching skills and curriculum content, leading to

3. Providing support as new knowledge and skills are implemented in the classroom and school

As we said earlier, implementation challenges us to redevelop content as we incorporate it into the process of teaching. We climb from the level of learning that we can obtain in the course or workshop and develop control over it as we incorporate it into our current practice. Here we need the support of others. Essentially, we need someone to talk to. That person does not need to study the innovative practice but does need to listen to plans and descriptions of effects as implementation is attempted.

Important—This person should *not* try to offer authoritative advice. Listening and commenting are sufficient. If the companion has little experience with the innovation, strong advice is not advisable.

4. Building an energizing and positive culture in the district and school

Good social climates draw individuals toward growth and provide a supportive atmosphere as they study curriculum and teaching and ways of modulating to their students and making partners of parents.

Educators flourish in positive cultures and struggle to grow where the climate is indifferent or worse. Building a positive ethos depends on strong and articulate leadership from the top down. The findings from the Iowa Association of School Boards study indicated that the elevating ethos touches everyone—that affirmation is radiated toward students, parents, teachers, principals, central office coordinators, and the superintendents and trustees. And affirmation is radiated by word and deed. Superintendents, board members, principals—the official leaders of the district—speak affirmatively about each other and generate initiatives to support others. And the teacher-leaders add their voices and treat students and parents as intelligent, positive citizens. Feeling the affirmation, parents and teachers respond in kind, relating warmly to the educators and putting out reciprocal energy. In both the Harkreader and Weathersby and Association of School Boards studies, the effect on achievement was more powerful than socioeconomic strata.

The key to supporting individuals is to create an elevating environment. Affirmative environments pay off, educationally speaking, in many ways. When teachers live in healthy schools, they create an elevating environment for their students.

5. Using systems for studying teaching to help teachers analyze teaching, make decisions about enhancing their repertoire, and do so

When someone watches himself or herself teach, what does that person see?

For one reason or another, most folks look at their teaching from an evaluative stance. They look at a communication and say, "This was good," or, "That was not so good." Possibly the evaluative stance comes from the years of growing up in schools, where so much student work—and behavior—is evaluated so regularly. However, the attempt to make a global judgment can obscure a lot of what is happening in the behavior of both the instructors and that of their students.

A few years ago, one of the most interesting—and effective— ways of helping teachers study their behavior and try to make productive changes in it occurred when the development of inexpensive videotaping was engineered. Essentially, one could now see oneself in interactive fields of endeavor: One could tape oneself, analyze the tape, and reflect on one's behavior. Whereas the use of analysis in the past had been the province of supervisors, now the practitioner could look at his or her own performance and that of the students and reflect on it.

In the 1960s and 1970s, many teacher education programs taught their teacher candidates and cooperating teachers to use a number of frames of reference to analyze their teaching (the most common, called "Interaction Analysis," was developed by Ned Flanders when a doctoral student at the University of Chicago). By 1970 there were about 50 observation systems (see Simon & Boyer, 1966), compiled in *Mirrors for Behavior (RBS)*. The systems focused on the verbal behavior of the teachers and students. As an illustration we will use the Teacher Innovator System (TIS), developed by Bruce and his colleagues at Teachers College, Columbia University (Joyce & Showers, 2002); Syracuse University (Berj Harootunian); and the Ontario Institute of Education at the University of Toronto (David Hunt). This system was developed to help teachers study their behavior and that of their students as they learned a repertoire of models of teaching and to study the relationship between the conceptual level of teachers (Harvey, Hunt, & Schroder, 1966) and their behavior in the classroom. TIS deals with three dimensions of verbal behavior: the handling of information (the cognitive levels with which information is surfaced and analyzed), structuring (the organization and administration of procedures), and sanctions (the approval of student ideas). The teacher records his or her interaction with the students, analyzes it, and makes decisions about moves to make to increase learning.

For example: Let us imagine that our Nancy has learned to use TIS to study her behavior and that of her students. Nancy is concerned that the students are not building concepts as well as she would like. She tapes several episodes where the content is the demography of a variety of nations, and she is trying to get them to analyze how the development of educational systems affects economic growth. In her analysis she watches the handling of information closely. She asks the students to clarify information about the countries ("How many children receive education and how much?" "Are there differences between boys and girls?") And then she asks them to compare the countries they are studying. ("How are they different?" "Do some educate more of their children?") As the students respond, she notices that they deal with the particular rather than the general. In other words, although the students are learning a great many facts, they are having trouble either classifying the nations or, possibly, need help in expressing concepts. Nancy decides that there may be a problem with language, and she plans a couple of sessions where she will concentrate on building the language of concepts. She gathers a set of teddy bears and has the students classify them. Size, color, texture, and expression, among other attributes, emerge. Then she asks them to describe their categories and works with them to speak conceptually about them.

Now, our Nancy is a very sophisticated teacher and brings her students into very interesting explorations in world geography. And with the help of videotape, she is able to focus on ways of building the students' learning capacity.

Our illustration is only one of many possibilities. Learning to study one's teaching and the learning behavior of one's students is facilitated by the use of a system for studying verbal behavior. Groups can use this technique also, but that is a story for another chapter (see Joyce, Brown, & Peck, 1981).

The Individual as a Neglected Species: Redressing the Situation

The fine learning capacity of teachers is well documented, as is the wide range in developed repertoire and needs. As investments are made in professional development, we believe that supporting teachers as individuals is critically important. And the health of teachers as individual learners is basic to the health of the other models of staff development. The more individuals learn, the more they have to share, the better they are able to learn new curricular and instructional repertoire, and the more discriminating they are in selecting workshops and courses.

Preface to Chapters Three, Four, and Five

Democracy, Charters, and Professional Development

We introduce the models on direct personal/professional service (Chapter 3), cooperative/collaborative models (Chapter 4), and curricular and instructional initiatives (Chapter 5) by recommending that school faculties develop and adopt a "charter" that specifies how the faculty (principal and teachers) will govern itself. Developing a charter can have a large effect on the social system of the school in such a way that mentoring, coaching, the development of professional learning communities, and curricular and instructional initiatives can flourish. We place this section here because we believe that the implementation of all approaches to professional development are uneven at present and can be improved dramatically if governance issues are settled as initiatives of any type are made.

To do well, all types of professional development inevitably depend on the social and organizational characteristics of schools and school districts. In some social climates, all models have a good chance to thrive and good odds for success. In some others, any model will fail to be richly implemented. Partly this is due to the energy brought to the situation by the staffs of the schools. As we discussed in Chapter 2, the ethos of a district and school has much to do with the health of its members, professional staff, and students and parents.

Here we concentrate on the improvement of the organizational climate of schools through a procedure that we call, thanks to Carl Glickman, a school "charter"—the creation of a democratic social system that is a fertile place for teachers' minds and skills and, not incidentally, for those of the students as well.

We will use the concept throughout the rest of the book as we try to give each approach a good shot at being effective and invigorating.

Although there have been a number of other frameworks for governing schools in a democratic fashion, during the late 1980s and 1990s, Carl Glickman and Emily Calhoun made democratic process and action research inquiry a hallmark of the League of Professional Schools, organized through the University of Georgia. The staffs of member schools created an actual document representing the institutionalization of a democratic process in the organization of the school (see Calhoun & Glickman, 1993).

In ordinary practice, how principals and teachers are to work together in governance is not usually spelled out in policies or dealt with when they are hired and placed in a school. Most faculty members will have experienced isolation and privatism in their previous schools or in student teaching. If a school is to be operated in a collaborative fashion, its faculty has to take steps to generate democracy in a profession where individualism is the tradition. We begin by illustrating what building a charter involves, beginning on day one of a new academic year.

Building a Charter

Let us imagine that we are observers in a school in a neighborhood where there are both homes and stores. The principal and staff are hired by the district central office, and, one day, the children are brought to school and registered. The staff comes to the school for an incredibly short period—often only a day or two—before the school opens in the fall. Most likely, textbooks and library books are still being unboxed as the first bike or bus arrives and the first bell rings.

The teachers deploy to their classrooms to greet the children and begin the first day. The principal and school secretary are very busy answering questions, getting bus routes modified, talking to nervous parents, registering latecomers, and ordering supplies for the cafeteria to make up for an earlier snafu in calculations.

A few days later, schooling has settled into familiar routines. The books are unpacked and more arrive and the central library begins to take shape. Classroom libraries appear, and students are taking books home. Parent meetings are held, and the parents visit the classrooms. Computers arrive, and the teacher workstations are installed with projection capability as well as Internet access, e-mail (from school to home if needed), electronic encyclopedias, talking dictionaries, and other necessities. Computers for students to use have not yet arrived, and how to deploy them is up in the air.

After about ten days Ms. Alicia Henry, the principal, sends a note to all the teachers that she would like a meeting on September 18, a Thursday, from 3 PM to 5 PM with refreshments and parents welcome afterwards, to discuss

1. immediate logistical problems and how to solve them,

2. the district calendar for the year,

3. a meeting with parents she will hold next week to welcome them and invite questions,

4. types of staff development needed soon (several staff have indicated that computer technology is an area of serious need), and

5. how to organize for ongoing school-improvement-oriented action research, including thinking about having a school steering committee to consider actions and lead them.

As the teachers anticipate the meeting, they are positive. They like the idea that Henry will be presiding over a gathering of the parents. Some indicate that they are not sure what "action research" means.

However, Ms. Henry receives a note from the office of the superintendent that district rules stipulate that no school-level meeting can be held before October, and then it can only be one hour long.

When she contacts the superintendent, he informs her that the rules were made by the board at the request of the previous superintendent. An additional rule is that the school can have only one meeting each month.

She remonstrates, indicating that leadership from her or from teachers will be completely stymied unless they can meet together.

Henry gathers the faculty together for a series of two-a-week brief meetings at noon (apparently legal in the district). Logistics occupy most of the first two meetings. Then, with their assent, she arranges that part of a planning day be given over to a meeting with a district computer technology staff member to assess whether she can provide what they need. In the fourth meeting, she deals with the general school improvement question and suggests that they build a charter—a kind of constitution—saying how they will govern themselves and how they propose to improve the school by increments, initially small but eventually of unknown magnitude. They discuss what this might mean and ask her to provide some items that might be included in an agreement.

A week or so later, she proposes that the staff first agree that if 80 percent of them approve, they will have a governance structure where

> They elect a steering committee that includes Alicia. All staff vote; the five teachers receiving the most votes are elected. A new steering committee is elected every two years.

> As an entity, they study ways of making small improvements and how to implement them—including solving small problems as they emerge.

> They study how to carry on schoolwide action research where the health of the school is studied continuously and they make initiatives to improve it as needed.

> And, if a major curricular/instructional change appears to be needed, it can be adopted if an 80 percent majority agrees.

On an 80 percent positive vote, this will be their charter.

(You will be interested to know that our experience is that when this type of process has been carried out with a charter similar to this, in most cases more than 80 percent voted for the charter. In many, the provisions were unanimously approved, and 90 percent or more was not unusual.)

If the staff approves the charter, Ms. Henry will take it to the board of education for their information and to ask for their approval to have more faculty meetings than the district schools normally have and more days or day-equivalents (three two-hour sessions equaling one day) that she can use for professional development. The superintendent is supportive.

Note that the figure 80 percent is used *twice*, first for the adoption of the charter and second for the adoption of any major school improvement initiative once the charter is in effect.

The Objectives

The primary objectives are to free the staff from the constraints of the norms that depress collective action—not the work rules but the norms of privatism and individualism that dominate the cultures of most schools. The idea is to liberate them to work together as a professional community whose members feed each other professionally and work together to develop initiatives that benefit the whole school.

We believe that the development of a charter is necessary so that the constraints of traditional norms do not prevent progress—the charter works to bring the entire staff together.

The board approves Ms. Henry's schedule for meetings and, subsequently, will approve her requests to augment the school budget to increase time available for staff development. The development of legitimacy for the charter and understanding by the central office personnel are important. Working through the organization and its rules and norms requires the ability to negotiate. She is sure to apply for grants and anticipates that time spent early on will pay off later as her faculty develops plans that alter normal procedures. One way to look at school improvement initiatives is that improvement in student learning will not take place *unless* procedures, including curriculum and instruction, are altered.

Time to get together is critical. Aside from the collaborative/ cooperative models for staff development and school renewal, there is a running agenda of issues requiring that information be spread throughout the staff and what we call a constant flow of "light housekeeping" tasks where collective discussion and decision making are best. Aside from the days of work opening and closing school, paid days for formal professional staff development and meetings add up to about five days per year or about 40 hours. Ordinarily these are scheduled as specific days. Suppose, however, that some are reconfigured into two-hour blocks scheduled every other week, or about 16 such periods.

With such an arrangement, there can be regular informational/ light housekeeping time and regular training, data collection, decision making, and support for implementation. Prodded by Ms. Henry, the board negotiates this "distributed time" option for schools that wish to have it.

The district has begun to approach the serious time problem. With a few more incremental changes, they can nurse staff development, school renewal, and the organizational climate into decent health.

A Note on Leadership

Where a schoolwide steering committee is formed, the principal is the *pro tem* chairperson, although leadership relative to various tasks devolves on the several faculty members. Committees within the school may be given specific responsibilities.

All aspects of making a charter work depend heavily on leadership by the principals. In addition to the duty of looking after the learning of the students and the learning environments of the school, they have duties relating to the staff. They are responsible for the professional health of the faculty as a whole and for looking after individuals. For example, they should be prepared to mentor new teachers, to help individuals and groups as they implement new skills, and to find the technical assistance to advance action research and the study of teaching skills.

The procedures described above are similar in an elementary, middle, or secondary school and in rural or urban settings. At all levels, priority is given to creating an affirmative environment where there is a continuous search for better ways of teaching and, therefore, opportunities for us to explore the rich landscape of educational practice.

3

Personal/Professional Direct Service Models

Helping People Do Their Thing

My biggest challenge is when I'm sure I'm right and my mentee is sure she's right.

—our reflective observer

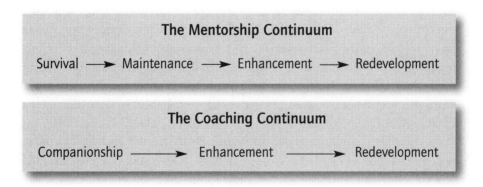

Here we discuss the largest complex professional development model ever organized in the United States. There are probably a great many participants in workshops on designated staff development days. Learning communities of groups of teachers in schools have become common. All teachers are visited by principals or district supervisors, some of whom coach the teachers intensively. But in terms of changes in roles and relationships, nothing like the organization of teachers to give one-on-one professional/personal support to other teachers has happened in the history of school improvement or professional development.

By *personal/professional service* we mean assigning an individual teacher to get to know another or several other teachers (possibly an entire school faculty), diagnose needs (with the teacher or teachers), and try to provide help in agreed-on professional areas. These are not informal friendships. What we characterize as personal/professional direct service models are formal programs. Currently, there are several types of them, all very large. In rough order of size, these are

- mentors for new teachers,
- generic coaches to school staffs,
- literacy coaches to school staffs, and
- coaches in other content areas staffs and individuals.

These services are in addition to those provided by principals, assistant principals, department heads, district central office staff, and the staffs of regional agencies.

This remarkable development has occurred from a combination of government actions and the intensive lobbying of national organizations, including the national and state offices of the teachers' union. In many states legislation has required that new teachers have a mentor for a year and, in many cases, for two years. In California, about 15,000 teacher candidates annually graduate from college and university preservice programs, and those programs depend on what have traditionally been referred to as cooperating teachers. Current legislation requires that new teachers have two years of mentoring after they take employment and that teachers moving to California from other states also have two years of mentoring. Not until the end of the second year does a novice teacher get a "clear" credential.

If mentors are classroom teachers who continue to teach classes, we would need 30,000 each year if each mentored one novice and 15,000 if each mentored two new teachers.

Coaching is also sizable. If full-time coaches were employed and each was assigned to an average of 10 teachers, we would need 300,000 nationally who, during their tenure as coaches, would have to be replaced by another teacher. Or, if they continued to teach students and each offered part-time coaching to a school staff, we would need as many as 100,000 to cover all school staffs. And reaching all staffs *is* the ambition of some of the national organizations.

There has got to be a reason for a movement of this size. The obstacles are formidable, yet many are being solved without the level of controversy and resistance that frequently accompany a simple school improvement initiative:

- To support coaching, school districts have to make serious budgetary decisions, even though federal programs like Reading First and Title I contribute funds (and, as they do so, press districts to recruit, train, and assign coaches). States generally support most of the direct costs of mentoring, but there are sizable ancillary costs.
- Moving this number of teachers from the classroom to mentoring or coaching duties has serious implications. And there are educational costs attendant to taking those who are regarded as the best teachers and assigning them either full- or part-time to support others.
- These roles are relatively new, and issues about preparation have to be faced. There are not thousands of experienced coaches and mentors queued up for the job—folks accustomed to showing up at a school and saying, "I'm here to help." And the expansion of mentoring of new teachers requires positions for persons who are not only believed to be effective teachers but who can develop strong relationships and successfully impart their lore to the novices. Seeking enough cooperating teachers to meet needs has always been difficult, but seeking tens of thousands of mentors and coaches is daunting. Nonetheless, these models of professional development are growing rapidly, and the major thorny logistical problems described above appear to be taken in stride in most settings. Let's take a close look at both of them, beginning with mentoring.

Mentoring: Variations on a Supportive Theme

We begin with the rationales for mentoring, consider what it should accomplish minimally, and then examine a hierarchy of objectives that can guide work with the mentees.

Rationales

On need—there are three related rationales for mentoring programs.

1. The fundamental argument is that teaching is complex, so much so that it takes several years to learn to teach knowledgeably and skillfully. Essentially, the preservice programs orient teacher candidates to schooling and teaching and to an introductory knowledge base. But following student teaching, another year or two is needed to learn how to manage a classroom, implement curriculums, and assess student learning. From this perspective, mentoring can shepherd the teacher candidates through the early months and years of practice, with the mentor tutoring the new teacher and complementary workshops providing additional information and routes to skill.

2. The second rationale focuses on defects in the culture of educators and school systems. Even after 30 years of intense publicity about the problems of new teachers and the development of inductive programs, most advocates of mentoring maintain that new teachers are often given the most difficult students and most difficult subjects, including multiple preparations, and poor settings—having to teach in multiple venues while more experienced teachers have home classrooms to which their classes come.

   Thus, mentors are seen as protective companions, reducing the poor treatment of novices where it occurs. They accomplish this officially by working with superintendents, central office staffs, principals, and department chairs and by taking leadership when the culture of veteran teachers has not been protective of their new colleagues.

3. A third rationale is to pull the level of teaching higher than current practice. Mentoring is increasingly seen as more than a vehicle for socializing new teachers into teaching as such but going beyond that level to help new teachers develop 21st-century teaching skills for students needing 21st-century learning skills and knowledge.

From these elements of rationale, mentoring in general has the goal of providing companionship, protecting the novices, and helping them develop good professional knowledge and skill and beyond.

General Effects to Be Expected

Fundamental is the development of competence. Mentored teachers should have superior skills. And mentoring should *reduce* attrition of new teachers. A good many do not make it through the first year of teaching—or the second, third, or fourth—and mentoring should affect this.

Levels of Mentoring

At the beginning of the chapter, we presented the following continuum of levels of mentorship programs. Moving from left to right, each level is incorporated into the next one. Although we will focus on the objectives and what the mentor does to achieve them, the good and better inductive programs have sets of seminars and workshops for both mentors and mentees. These generally focus on basic teaching skills, more advanced models of teaching, and curriculum content and materials, as well as processes of mentoring and studying teaching.

Survival/Basic Competence

This level focuses on the tendency of *new teachers* to feel overwhelmed by the problems of navigating classroom management and teaching. The mentor provides companionship, helps explain the curriculum and how to teach it, and, if needed, works with the administration and other teachers to eliminate hardship conditions and build relationships with the new arrival.

Maintenance

This level works on helping the candidate organize the curriculum areas, gather materials, assess student learning, and learn to use basic cooperative learning strategies. The survival and maintenance levels can be carried out simultaneously. The novice is learning to handle the situation, manage the students, and instruct and assess at a level at least equal to the norms in the school.

Enhancement

The mentor (and workshops and seminars) introduces the teacher candidate to more sophisticated models of teaching. These include the basic inductive and concept attainment models and the more complex cooperative learning skills.

The goal is to help the new people reach a level above the norm. Workshops and coaching by the mentor are generally combined to bring new practices into the repertoire of the novice, including ways of assessing higher-order cognitive and social outcomes. Mentors can provide companionship and technical support as the mentees implement an increasing array of curricular and instructional strategies.

Redevelopment

At this level mentoring takes on the look of a school improvement program.

The mentor and mentee study 21st-century teaching and learning models and implement them, including assessing student learning. The mentee has progressed from good to excellent to outstanding!

Critical Issues and Considerations in the Development of Mentoring Programs

Developing programs is a multisided affair, and there are issues to be dealt with—total agreement has not been achieved in every area where decisions have to be made.

Selecting Mentors

Mentors work by nurturing and instruction. They provide emotional support by nurturing and point the way to managing the classroom and teaching effectively by instructing. They teach the new teacher. The demands at each level are somewhat different.

Survival/basic competence mode. Mentors need to be solid teachers and warm and supportive. They need to be oriented toward making friends with strangers (their mentees) and willing to play an advocacy role when necessary.

Maintenance. Mentors need to have a repertoire that provides options for engaging in the basic tasks of teaching. They possess a variety of tools to relate to students and teaching strategies for accomplishing higher-order and lower-order goals. As at the other levels, they need warmth and affirmativeness and a willingness to advocate.

Enhancement. Now the mentor's range of tools needs be larger, and mentors need good skills for helping mentees learn new things as well.

Redevelopment. Now, in addition to the foregoing, our mentor needs to be willing to learn new curricular and instructional models and team up so that the mentee learns them as well. The mentor program needs to provide the opportunity to add to curricular and teaching repertoires.

Full or part time? From the same school or not? There are debates about these questions. We lean toward keeping mentors in their classrooms and assigning each to no more than two mentees. Our primary reason has to do with demonstration, which is much easier and more powerful in one's own venue. And we continue to have their services with children. They can teach in the same school or come from another.

Most advocates, however, prefer full-time mentors assigned to a dozen or so new teachers. There is no research on this subject, and we are not sure that a definitive study could be designed.

Full-time mentors can be very effective and get the opportunity to reach a good many students through their teachers. Most will want to employ video demonstrations to teach to their entire coterie rather than demonstrating in each classroom. We think a "caseload" of about ten is plenty.

Is there a pool of potential mentors (and coaches)? The personal/professional service models rest on the assumption that there are skilled and knowledgeable teachers who have much to offer new and experienced teachers, have or can acquire the tools to do so, are willing to help others, and can be released for several years from all or a portion of their teaching duties. Thirty years of experience with mentoring and ten with coaching give us reason to believe that all of these are true. There are top professionals who can and are willing to help others. The organizational arrangements have been proven to require some changes that are not always easy to bring about, but they can be achieved.

The mentor/supervisor/assessor/administrator complex. The major teachers' organizations are often adamant that teachers who assume roles as coaches and mentors *not* play any role in assessment and evaluation—those are the province of supervisors. For example, in California, where the districts award the clear credential (universities awarding only the preliminary credential), the mentors will know the most about the teacher candidate. It is unlikely that their knowledge will not be transmitted to some extent, but there is a real official conundrum to be solved. In California today it is *illegal* for mentors and principals to share information that might be used in assessment of teacher competence. In New York, on the other hand, if local districts work it out with the local union, information can be shared.

Supervisionlike behavior. Less discussed is the role of supervision-like behavior in the roles of mentor and coaches. Mentors and coaches have to approach the task of getting to know their clients in ways familiar to supervisors who have the same role. This is a complex issue—is the function of the mentors actually supervision without the formal assessment role that resides in official supervisors? In practice, we'll find more overlap than the unions would like.

An analogous issue is whether persons with supervisory respon-sibilities can *also* provide mentoring services. Several times in this book we have asserted, and will do so again here, that supervisors *can* certainly mentor a new or experienced teacher. In fact, doing so is an important part of their job. The notion that mentors or coaches cannot deal with evaluation of a teacher is one thing. That principals or cen-tral office personnel cannot be a mentor or coach *because* they have supervisory responsibilities is quite another thing. We cannot accept the idea that the head of the school, or a leadership group, or central office personnel cannot help the new teacher or, for that matter, the more experienced teacher who needs help.

Mentor as protector. Although we dealt with this topic briefly in the summary of rationales for mentoring, a further consideration is worthwhile. We have to say that we are shocked that bad treatment of novice teachers still occurs. Until recently we believed that the old practice of giving the new teacher the struggling students and the smallest classroom was far in the past (*it certainly is passé where we work!*); then we realized that many of the current books on mentoring suggest that the practice is still common. That stimulated us to con-duct some interviews, and, shockingly, we found that there are still set-tings where the novices are treated badly—and their students as well.

Here is a list of the cruelties supplied by one of the more promi-nent authors (Sweeny, 2008), who writes about mentoring teacher candidates and novice teachers.

The new teacher is given . . .

1. the most preparations of any role on the staff;

2. multiple school sites (this is a district/central office problem);

3. multiple classrooms—what we call the "migrating" classroom;

4. classrooms stripped of resources (cannibalized by the neigh-boring staff);

5. the most difficult and challenging students; and

6. multiple extra-duty assignments.

And, they often have to take courses to complete certification or meet the special requirements of a district.

This and similar lists are used to justify in part the need for mentors who can try to "protect" the new teacher from being victimized.

If a district follows such scurrilous practices as those in this list, then we do not believe that a mentor program is in order. Administrators who engage in such practices should be disciplined—probably demoted. Mentorship is not the avenue for correcting such abuses. And mentors cannot thrive in their role in a district or school that tolerates such practices. Because novices—and their students—have been treated badly in some backward school systems, teachers' organizations should be vigilant and take whatever action is necessary to correct the situation. In large secondary schools, department heads have major responsibility for determining the conditions for new teachers. Principals have the responsibility for overseeing practice.

We have come to believe that school charters may need to include provisions to ensure optimal conditions for new teachers—and the place of mentors in the working culture of the school.

In mentoring, agreements need to made that new teachers will *not* be given the most difficult students, most preparations, and poorest rooms and facilities. Rather, they will be given normal classes, fewer preparations, and good facilities. If not on the faculty, the mentor will be welcomed as a part-time member of the staff, and other teachers will come together to support the new professionals. Principals will support the new teachers with a caring relationship, counsel, and observation and advice. In a small school, the principal may be the mentor.

Research on Mentoring Is Badly Needed

A large-scale study piggybacked on the National Assessment program investigated whether the connection of mentors with novice teachers reduced attrition, and it did not (Smith & Ingersall, 2004).The most complex form of mentoring programs involves giving information to principals so that they can cooperate in helping the mentee and sets of workshops for the novice teachers. This complex form, which was rarely used, reduced attrition somewhat. The design did not permit learning whether the workshops, rather than the mentoring relationship, might have been responsible.

Another Note on Mentees and Attrition

New teachers are somewhat older than many people expect. In California, internship programs graduate 25 percent of beginning teachers, and according to data from Michael McKibbin, director of the internship programs for the Commission for Teacher Preparation and Licensing, their *average* age is 36. Many have had years of experience in other fields. And officials at the Commission believe that the average age of the 15,000 teachers who graduate each year from college and university programs is about 31. The average graduate of career change-oriented programs is 35 years old (McKibbin, personal communication, March 2008).

Thus, many mentees are experienced and mature adults with considerable knowledge of the society. They are *not* 21-year-olds thrown into difficult schools to sink or swim. If they *are* thrown in, they are still experienced adults.

Attrition: Is Some a Good Thing?

The current literature regards attrition as a nearly totally bad thing and one produced by an unsupportive environment. That may not be the whole story about attrition.

We suspect that a good many teacher candidates will stop at the point where they have the preliminary credential—that is, they will not apply for work in teaching. A number of others will put their toes in the water for a few months or a year and then pull their feet back. Thus, the often-stated object of mentoring—to help new teachers stay in teaching by better managing the complexity of the job and the sometimes terrible conditions they are put in—may not be the whole story. Some newly credentialed people may have decided, during teacher training, that they do not wish to teach. And, heresy here, some new teachers might well be happier in another line of work. That someone tries teaching and then leaves it may not be a bad thing for everyone who makes that choice. Some sources indicate that, *without mentoring*, only about 10 or 15 percent of new teachers leave teaching after their first year. That small number might actually be a good thing, for them at least. New teachers who are ambivalent about teaching can legitimately test the waters, and mentoring may have much less influence than their own assessment about whether "teaching is for them."

Also, a number of teacher candidates may simply *not* be well-suited to the circumstances of classroom teaching. We have known quite a few literacy-oriented teachers who were repelled by the classroom-management side of teaching and went on to other things. We find no fault in that.

In addition, some people get through teacher education programs before it becomes apparent that they do not have the combination of personal characteristics that is needed for teaching. That they weed themselves out is better than the alternatives.

At times mentors may be riding in a race that is already run and the outcome due to factors out of their control.

Coaching: Further Variations on a Supportive Theme

We will begin with rationale, then proceed to the three levels in the continuum, and then discuss issues and considerations as programs for coaching are developed.

Rationales

The needs for generic coaches and coaches in literacy and other curriculum areas are expressed in similar terms as those for mentors.

1. Improving student achievement is fundamental. While the most-mentioned concerns supporting mentoring are socialization into teaching *as is* and mitigating the problems attendant on poor treatment of novices, the case for coaching rests on improving student achievement. This can be done by providing service designed to bring everyone up to snuff or by focusing on the elevation of general or subject-related practice.

2. Second is that, to achieve 21st-century levels of achievement, many teachers need to improve their knowledge and teaching skills. From this perspective, coaching becomes an avenue for modernizing the curriculum and can morph into general school improvement initiatives. Many of the documents supporting the use of coaches in mathematics simultaneously emphasize coaching to ensure the development of traditional basic skills and curriculum reform.

3. Third is the proposition that some teachers have exemplary knowledge and skills that are teachable to others and that they would like to help their colleagues. In addition, they know how to provide assistance and/or are willing to study how to do so. That assistance can include helping colleagues engage in personal and collaborative inquiry into teaching and learning.

Effects to Be Expected

The overall goal is to help professionals develop better skills and knowledge, either across the curriculum areas or in a particular one—literacy being the most prominent at the present time. The degree of change can range from acquiring or polishing basic teaching skills to the implementation of new curricular components and even to the development of action research for school improvement.

At the beginning of the chapter, we presented this continuum—it has noticeable similarities to the continuum of mentoring programs.

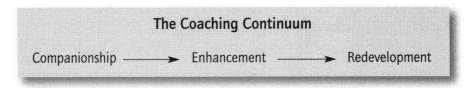

The Coaching Continuum

Companionship ———→ Enhancement ———→ Redevelopment

Again, we see types of service with increasing complexity that are consistent with the levels of objectives. They range from providing a companionable environment to enhancing repertoire to developing outstanding capability.

Companionship

Essentially companions provide support through the development of a nurturant rapport. Within it a teacher can examine his or her practice and the response of the students and make decisions about making positive changes. The creation of a social space that is both safe and analytic is at the center of the process. And both coach and coached spend time reflecting together on practice and how to improve it.

Enhancement

As in mentoring, coaching programs at this level seek not only to polish current practices but to elevate them to a standard of excellence. Through workshops and the coaching relationship, new strategies for managing the classroom and teaching and assessing learning are introduced. With the help of the coach, the teacher implements the new content and, reflecting on student learning, seeks to elevate it.

Redevelopment

Again as in mentoring, at this level coaching begins to become leadership for school improvement.

Both parties study 21st-century teaching and learning models and implement them, including assessing student learning. The goal is outstanding, forward-looking performance.

Critical Issues and Considerations in the Development of Coaching Programs

The development of a program involves some of the same decisions as in the case of mentoring models, but additional decisions must be made because entire staffs of experienced teachers are involved.

Selecting Coaches

All coaches need to be good, solid instructors and affirmative managers of students. And willingness to provide help to others is essential. At the higher levels, a greater repertoire of teaching strategies is important, as well as the desire to inquire into teaching and master new curricular and instructional models.

Most coaches need professional development that helps them learn how to engage with new colleagues and how to learn new material. Assigning teachers to coach entire school faculties is a relatively new practice, and organizers need to realize that they, as well as the coaches and school staffs, will have to learn many new things and procedures may have to be modified—*will, in fact, have to be modified, possibly several times*—before optimal ones are found.

Full- or part-time? From the same school or not? As in the case of mentoring, for service to individual teachers, we lean toward keeping coaches in their classroom and assigning them to no more than two teachers. Again, our primary reason has to do with demonstration, which is much easier and more powerful in one's own venue. And the coaches continue to use their services with children. They can teach in the same school or come from another.

However, coaches assigned to schools need to be full-time and be assigned to one school where they have not taught.

The clients of coaching. School faculties and their teachers are the clients. They are not identical—it takes time and effort to figure out where coaching might begin.

And the clients come with various social climates and states of growth.

There will be *omnivores* and *active consumers*; some of them are at the top of their profession before the coach arrives. Generally, they will be glad to welcome a good colleague.

Passive consumers will be acquiescent but friendly, but finding out their needs can take work—they will tend to let the coach do the decision making.

Reticent consumers will ward off support. Coaches need to learn that their off-putting manner is not personal—they are "that way" with everybody.

Feeding the omnivores the best you can is a good strategy. There will be plenty for everyone.

Implementation Needs

Funding a program and assigning state and district coordinators is the easy part—much easier than implementation. We will deal here with just two aspects of implementation—preparing coaches and preparing schools.

Preparing coaches. The experts on mentoring and coaching, particularly those who have been mentors and coaches, are agreed that a considerable amount of effort needs to be put into training. Successful programs include have what amounts to courses for all parties.

Coaching of schools has not been around as long as mentoring of new teachers, but the history has brought participants and observers to the same conclusion—coaches need more training than was originally envisioned, training of the same magnitude as mentors. And, where a particular curriculum area is involved, intensive training in that area, such as literacy, is vital. In our own projects, where support personnel provide training and coaching, for two to three years those people receive 10 to 15 days of formal training each year, meet weekly or more often, and study implementation and student learning on a formative basis. And they always feel they should have more.

Preparing schools: Paving the way with the charter. We believe that building a charter or its equivalent is very important if either mentoring or coaching programs are to thrive. Once a charter is in place, the mentoring and coaching programs need to be considered by the school faculties and voted on.

Agreeing to have a schoolwide generic or curriculum area coach—and by an 80 percent vote or better—is critical to the success of the coaching program. The faculty members will be agreeing to be observed and to have discussions about teaching—*their* teaching. They will be agreeing to learn more strategies and more curricular and instructional models. If they don't make these agreements in advance, staff members can feel free to avoid coaching, attendance at workshops, and collective efforts to improve curriculum and teaching. Also, the faculty, including the principal, should interview potential coaches, and both coach and faculty should agree that they have a good match.

Without these procedures, assigning a "coach" to go to a school, introduce himself or herself to the principal and faculty, and start to build helping relationships is a recipe for failure.

The Work of Coaches and Mentors

Although both induction programs and service to experienced teachers include seminars and workshops and networking meetings, the roles of mentor and coach are the fulcrums of these movements. Here we will examine advice given by national organizations and experts in these models to coaches and organizers of coaching programs. Most of this applies to mentoring as well.

We need to acknowledge the work of Bean and Deford in their *Dos and Don'ts for Literacy Coaches* (2008). We used their sequence of advice to guide much of this section. We will alternate quotes and paraphrased sentences from their book.

Definitions, Rationale, Implementation, and Conditions of Work

Let us begin with the statement that the term *coach* is a colloquial, general term as used today. What is important is the core of the initiatives that, in mentoring and coaching, are bringing thousands of practitioners to serve their peers. Our focus here is on the category called *literacy coaches*. A clear rationale is that their service is justified by the needs of teachers in the general literacy area. Above the primary grades, literacy has not been included as part of teachers' general preparation to teach the core curriculum subjects. However, as many literacy coaches are assigned to the primary grades, the rationale is that the primary teachers also need additional help in the teaching of reading and writing. Generic coaches work across the core curriculum areas and elementary school grade levels. If one understands the role of the literacy coach, one only needs to think across the curriculum to understand the generic role.

In the next pages we key off the thorough presentation by Bean and Deford (2008), experts on coaching, to discuss a set of issues related to the process of coaching. We intersperse their advice to coaches with our comments on the topics and issues they deal with. Our comments are indented.

Bean and Deford (2008) begin with the statement that "literacy coaches are assuming a range of complex tasks within schools" (p. 1). They go on to mention instructional planning, assessment of students, talking to teachers about instruction, and coaching—observing, demonstration teaching, and discussing instruction in relation to the demonstrations and observations.

From their examination of the literature and interviews with coaches, they have developed a set of guides for new coaches that are echoed in the rest of the relevant literature. They begin with . . .

> *Introduce yourself and your role.* The new coach needs to talk to the principal and "take a few minutes to talk at a faculty meeting" and distribute a flyer. Many small-group meetings are needed to enable teachers to say what they need and to hear what the coach brings to the equation.

> > *We comment:* Again, we believe that the development of a charter should precede a *decision by the school faculty* that a coach is needed. The leadership team should interview candidates, select one or two, and then introduce the new staff member to the faculty and take responsibility for integrating the coach into the operation of the school. Without a charter, the entire faculty should vote on whether to find a coach and invite that person to the school.

> *Bean and Deford advise:* "*Work with all teachers.*" The coach needs to contact everybody and not to fall into an easy trap, which is to work only with those who are most amenable to the process. They bring up an issue that is virtually oxymoronic. "One of the quickest ways to reduce teacher interest is for the teachers to think the coach is there to 'fix them up' as if they are not doing their jobs or are considered to be weak. This FIXIT approach breeds fear, resentment, and resistance. Coaches who find themselves in this predicament have a difficult time working as a colleague with teachers" (p. 2).

> > *We comment:* They pose a real oxymoron. The coach is assigned to the school because the teachers need help in the literacy area, but the coach is to convince the teachers that they are really OK. For mentors this problem is not as severe because the difference in

experience makes the difference in their roles obvious, but some new teachers can resist help as fiercely as a hard-bitten veteran. The coach is there to help, but the teachers may believe they are in fine shape without the help.

That is another reason we like the charter. The teachers acknowledge the need and help select the coach.

Sensibly, Bean and Deford advise: Work first to establish a relationship of trust. All the experts bring this up, and, usually, the coach is seen to have the major responsibility.

> Again, we believe that the integration of the coach into the faculty is the responsibility of the staff, not the coach. We make much of the need for schools to establish understandings about participation in initiatives. If the charter specifies that when the faculty votes overwhelmingly to take a particular course in relation to literacy, then a coach can be engaged to help the staff work on their literacy skills.
>
> In some cases described in the literature, the coach is assigned to the school, presumably by the district central office, and then must work himself or herself into the good graces of each faculty member. That is a daunting task. In a bad case, the coach is pressed to accept the staff's reason why achievement is low: It is not a product of poor instruction but a consequence of poor parenting, a poor neighborhood, and the characteristics of the (again poor) students. There are schools where all the classroom doors are locked! Not locked against the coach, just locked. *And* where all the little windows in the doors are covered with layers of construction paper. *And* where the principal, in an introductory visit through the school, says things like "Let's not go there. She doesn't like to be observed." Changing those conditions should not be the job of a new coach working with strangers but is the task of the district supervisors, who have authority as well as persuasiveness.

Again, Bean and Deford's (2008) specificity and sensibility are useful. In their view the coach needs to . . .

"Listen carefully."

We agree: Yes, we should listen to the folks we hope to help.

Maintain confidentiality.

Yes. Don't spill the beans to those who evaluate. Some exponents believe that teachers are concerned that the mentor or coach might be a spy for assessors. In our view, few people would agree to spy. Those who would should not be coaches. In California, it is actually illegal for a mentor to discuss a mentee with a principal.

Bean and Deford stress something that can have surprising complexity if it is to be done well: *Work from teachers' agendas.*

> We agree, with a "but." Clearly, one wants to take the teachers' frame of reference into account—like by asking what they might want to learn. However, the mentor or coach is there precisely to help teachers progress beyond their own frame of reference. Asking people what they want to learn when you are there to try to influence them to do something different is an intricate task.

And, they urge: *Be positive.*

> This is an old saw, but an important one. In the words of experienced psychological counselors, "Sugar works a lot better than vinegar." If you look at another practitioner, you may find behavior that you would like to correct. Don't start there. Find what feels good and build on it. Eventually you can get around to some less fine behaviors, but do so in the context of helping the educator learn new and more effective teaching strategies.

Be assiduous about follow-through.

> In our careers, we have found this to be remarkably important. *Follow-through* in this context means living up to agreements of various sorts. If you say you will be there, be there! If you will provide certain kinds of materials, provide them! Teachers are very sensitive about whether agreements are kept. On the other hand, you are not their servant. You do your best.

Work with your administrator.

> The principal and school leadership team are important keys to the success of the coach. Essentially, the principal and coach work together to ensure the success of curriculum and instruction. There is no question about the importance of this support.
>
> We are glad that Bean and Deford support this. Some "experts" treat principals as an alienated species whose shortcomings the coach has to overcome.

The Literacy Coaches Clearinghouse, a joint project of IRA and NCTE, includes in its newsletter a sidebar of advice from a coach to new coaches. The advice has included putting your office away from the principal's so you won't be confused with administration. The author noted that she put her desk next to the bathrooms where she could "coach" while teachers waited for their students to do their business.

Now, we see no reason to ask a "coach" to run a gamut like that.

They warn against treating teachers from a stereotypic point of view: *Recognize—and appreciate—differences among teachers and how they work.*

We agree with this, but again with a small "but." There are whole books on this subject. Their import is that teachers have their own personalities and have generated their own personal styles of teaching. The admonition to learn about them and modulate the coaching/mentoring approach to them captures the title we have given to this family of models: personal/professional approaches. The coach is seen as the one who studies the client and carefully respects individual differences and modulates to them. Sometimes the teacher is seen as a somewhat fragile person who is accommodated to rather than accommodating of the coach. Rather than an impersonal professional who is offering service impersonally, the coach is almost in a therapeutic role.

As we indicated earlier, teachers come from all states of growth. If someone is off-putting, it may be that the person is generally reticent. The behavior may have nothing to do with the coach or the concept of coaching. And a gourmet omnivore may be ahead of the coach in many areas.

Bean and Duford elaborate on the point about paying attention to the client: *Recognize your own beliefs and attitudes about teaching and learning.*

This is a companion to the advice given above. The coach is to offer help in areas of need but is not a bulldozer. Rather, the coach is to work from self-awareness of his or her style and preferences, leading from strength but carefully.

And, sensibly: *Be a learner.*

This one pretty much goes without saying. One of the advantages of the coaching/mentoring role is that one is continuously trying on perspectives and finding areas for personal growth. A curiosity in the role is that every teacher, including ones who are poor at teaching literacy, does some things that the skilled literacy teacher can learn from. To this day, after we have observed literally thousands of teachers and offered training to a huge number, we will visit a classroom and see something we can add to our repertoire or use as a good illustration in a training session. Coaches will learn a good bit about teaching, unless they fall into the pit of thinking they are complete.

Let the data lead!

Throughout the literature the advocates of coaching/mentoring stress that a core practice is to observe and analyze and develop the intervention from the actual situation rather than developing a set approach that assumes that the client somehow needs it. This is another tricky area. The coach needs to work from his/her strength without assuming that everyone needs the same treatment.

Don't evaluate teachers. Evaluation "limits teachers' acceptance of them [coaches] and their role" (Bean & Deford, 2008, p. 4).

In other words, a helping relationship is incompatible with an evaluative function. Bean and DeFord stress that principals need to understand this and not co-opt the coach into giving them information about the teacher. They suggest that if a principal sees something that needs attention, he or she should mention it to the teacher. "The teacher should then be the one to contact the coach."

We add that principals should to continue to visit teachers and offer help and not drop the role of instructional leader because coaches are also studying the teachers and helping them. And, principals *can* be instructional leaders. In small schools in small districts, they can be the primary literacy trainer in their school and others. Some of the best trainers we have ever worked with are principals. As are some of the best nurturers of new teachers. Writing off 150,000 principals and assistant principals would be a terrible mistake. Don't fall into the trap of acting like the "expert."

The consensus is that the coaches need to work collaboratively with the teachers and that, if they position themselves as expert, they will be asked to provide solutions to problems rather than thinking through solutions *with* the teacher.

We like the collaborative mode, but one has to be careful. If a teacher is shooting himself or herself (and the students) in the foot with a poor practice, one may have to be direct and suggest an alternative.

The last point reveals the lessons of experience: *Don't jump in and expect immediate change.*

From their interviews the investigators concluded that new coaches greatly underestimated the time that change would take and felt "burned out" (their words) if their advice did not result in immediate change.

If you want rapid change, pick things that can change rapidly.

In Sum, What Can Be Expected From Coaches? Mentors?

The answer is . . . a large variety. This family of models defines a huge movement, and the personnel recruited will vary widely and, perhaps more important for variance, the schools, principals, and staffs will vary enormously. This is the first time that such a large school improvement initiative has been attempted. There is little programmatic research, and the results will have to be assayed over time.

Standardization: How Loose Should the Tether Be?

Consensus from both advocates and disinterested observers is that practice within these models varies widely. In all areas—selection, placement, training, and actual implementation behavior—standardization would be a foreign concept. *And that is not necessarily a bad thing.* The very core of the beliefs that rationalize this movement supports individual practice, as contrasted with the history of support initiatives such as clinical supervision, where disseminators of teaching practices were trained to a standard and expected to use it. Thus, the mentors and coaches, whether working with novices or school faculties, are to use their knowledge of practice and their skills in imparting that knowledge as best they can in the situation where they find themselves.

We will find criticism of this diversity. The critics complain that mentors or coaches vary so much in their practices. Our answer is that they *should* be quite different from one another. The whole point of these models would be lost if they were trained to a cookie-cutter way of working. However, "standards" for coaches are published, which apparently reflect the view that practice should be controlled to some extent, probably through training. "Most observers agree that reading coaches provide a powerful form of professional development—if they are skilled enough to meet coaching's varied demands" (IRA, 2004, p. 30). We think the answer to their problem is good professional development for the coaches—development that gives them strength in such a way that it capitalizes on their individuality.

As we state regularly, teachers as a whole are very resilient. They are not fragile—they can cope with change and easily handle the strain of new learning. A coach who knows how to teach literacy to children will find a capable learning machine on the other end of the transaction. Some (our dear reticent) will resist learning, but that is to be expected and not to be dwelt upon. No coach should be expected to reach every teacher in a collaborative relationship, nor should every principal. Stubborn adults can be *very* stubborn.

Most folks are really pleasant and are happy to improve their knowledge and skills. Teachers as a whole are a fine population to work with, and we have had the pleasure of working with several thousand of these decent folks.

4

Collaborative and Cooperative Models

The Pursuit of Synergy

Doing everything in a group would drive me crazy. But some things absolutely require collective inquiry and action.

—our reflective observer

We move now to models distinguished by cooperative study by small groups or the entire school or district faculty.

Caveat

Again, we remind ourselves about the tiny investment in professional development and the consequent limitations of the small allotments of time for either professional development or school improvement activities. We also remind ourselves of the nature of the workplace of educators. Individual educators are assigned space and students, and in most schools the space is physically separated from that of the other educators. Teachers' work is autonomous for the most part. Because they are assigned in such a way that they have responsibility from the beginning to the end of the day, getting teachers together in groups for any reason is difficult. Meeting times for groups have to be developed, or collaborative/cooperative approaches will flounder. And, we need to remember that groups are made up of individuals who bring their own states of growth to the table.

Definition

Bringing faculty members together to reflect on the education they are providing and to seek ways of making it better is the core of this family of models. A small faculty can be a learning community. Because synergy develops best in small groups (four or five members is big enough), a faculty can be composed of several study groups. Cross-grade and cross-disciplinary groups are preferred—the long history of research on cooperative learning supports the benefits of heterogeneity over homogeneity in group membership. Members need to come with the understanding that synergy leads to change— and that means change in themselves of a kind that is likely to bene- fit the students. Nearly always, productive change in education is an improvement in what is taught, how it is taught, or the social climate of the school.

Our (Meaning the Authors') Expectations for the Consequences of Inquiring in Study Groups—Professional Learning Communities

Teachers who think and study together can make positive changes that, moreover, *can make a serious difference in student learning in a relatively short time*. A change in curriculum and instruction that will make a difference to student learning begins to do so when it is implemented. A change that does not make a difference rapidly is unlikely to do so later (Joyce, Weil, & Calhoun, 2009).

Varieties and Varying Purposes

Let's begin *our* inquiry by identifying the cooperative/collaborative models that are most common in practice and in the literature. Importantly, cooperative/collaborative models can originate from any level of the organization. A group of teachers can form a learning com- munity. A school staff can decide to generate learning communities. A district can do so. Even a state can develop learning communities, as we will see in the next chapter in a project that brought together teams from 50 schools in one state.

Types of Collaborative Models

Whereas literature focusing on individuals is sparse, there is a great deal of literature on professional staff development generated within groups of teachers, often called "study groups" or "professional learning communities." The recommended procedures vary quite a bit as implementation occurs in various sites, but the common objective is to organize groups, and sometimes the faculty as a whole, to learn from one another's repertoires, study student learning, and build their stock of professional tools.

The most prominent types include

Open-process action research, guided by general principles, by the entire school staff, organized into groups within the school—Open process simply means that the general purpose is known, but the groups develop their own specific procedures. Some approaches begin by introducing particular articles and books to the groups (as in Murphy & Lick, 2005), influencing the content studied early, while others begin with a canvas of opinion about areas to be studied and whether to begin with the collection of perceptual data (the views of faculty members) or with the literature.

Open-process study by independent groups within the school—In many cases, groups are made up of volunteers. Individual faculty members are free not to participate. This version is common because of two assumptions by some organizers: first, that some (perhaps many) staff members will not want to participate and, second, that they should not be pressured to do so. Otherwise, the pooling of knowledge is believed to be sufficient to enable the participants to grow.

Disciplined action research by individuals, groups, or the entire faculty— This classic paradigm involves locating problem areas, collecting data, studying relevant literature, deciding to take action, and studying the results, perhaps modifying the action as a result. The entire faculty can participate, but small groups can conduct action research (see Sagor, 1992, where small groups are emphasized, and Calhoun, 1994, where whole-school varieties are described). When used with the entire school faculty, the overriding objective is to improve student learning. The means is to develop a democratic community and to generate disciplined, scientific procedures to study the school, its curriculum, and its community. Ultimately, exponents wish to see a self-renewing organization.

Districtwide action research—This is rare, but happens. It is impractical in huge districts simply because of the size and complexity of the organization. The assumptions are the same as with the schoolwide action research, but the scale is much larger. We have been partners in districts as large as 50 schools, but in districts of even a dozen schools, the demands on the superintendency and key central office leaders are exceptional. Clusters of schools (as secondary schools and their "feeder" elementary and middle schools) are workable.

Rationale

The cooperative/collaborative family is based on the following theses.

That collective energy (synergy)

1. *Increases positive affect*—People feel better about their participation, themselves, the content of events, and their colleagues. Here we have a consistent finding from research on cooperative models in general—they generate positive affect for the participants. The good feelings have a nice side effect; faculties that feel good generally pass the feelings along to their students.

   The cooperative learning studies include college students and other emerging young adults (see Johnson & Johnson, 2000). Our own informal studies with school improvement and staff development initiatives confirm that the collaborative activity does bring smiles to the faces of many people. Colleagues appreciate and enjoy the opportunity to talk to each other about their work.

2. *Increases learning of selected knowledge and skill*—The skills and knowledge are identified by the groups. The more groups reach beyond their existing repertoires, the more they need to anticipate needing training from outside their membership. Importantly, however, an energetic and focused group of educators can generate new learning for themselves that will eventually affect student learning, and there are many cases where that has happened (see Schmoker, 2004). In our own work as described in Chapters 5 and 7, teams have made large differences

in the implementation of new procedures, the study of effects on student learning, and results in terms of serious gains in student achievement.

3. *Increases implementation of knowledge and skills*—If a group, including a whole school faculty, determine to implement their selected approaches, they should have good odds.

When evaluating these models, the important question is not "Can they work?" but "What are the odds that they will work in a given setting with a certain amount of support?"

A Closer Look

Let's examine some of our variety of cooperative/collaborative models a little more closely, remembering that there are a dozen books or even more describing some of them and offering advice on how to do them well. We will glance at the open-ended approach—by definition, procedures are not specified but are left to the groups to develop. Then we will look more closely at action research for two reasons—it can stand alone or become a natural evolution from the less-structured practice. We have the most experience with the structured action research model and, therefore, have a richer storehouse of examples to draw on.

Open-Ended Approach

- Open-ended study groups and professional learning groups can involve whole schools and voluntary small groups.
- Open-ended study groups (professional learning communities) are probably the most disseminated of the collaborative/ cooperative options. As near as we can tell, volunteer groups are the most often recommended options.

The major assumption (read Mike Schmoker, 2004, a very articulate and wise disseminator of open-ended approaches) is that, if you gather a group of teachers together and have them study their practice and its effects, their collective knowledge and skills overlap to the point where each can learn from the others' practice. The primary mechanism is discussion and, often, study of students' work, with some visitation to one another's classrooms where the teachers can explain their practices to one another. Some schools have done very well with it, but the jury is still out on effects with large numbers of schools. As mentioned earlier, the Murphy/Lick (2005) approach begins by having the teachers study articles. Whether that helps is not clear, but the approach itself is straightforward—it requires consultants who have developed packages of articles designed to get thinking going.

Hord and Sommers (2008) describe what they call tenets—elements of productive groups:

- Shared beliefs, values, and vision
- Shared and supportive leadership
- Collective learning and its application
- Supportive conditions
- Shared personal practice

We add another essential—a drive to increase student learning through the addition of teaching repertoire.

Action Research for Individuals, Small Groups, and Schools

Up to a point, the action research processes are virtually the same whether individuals, small groups, or entire faculties are involved, but the whole-school version involves the development of democratic decision making, a common focus throughout the organization, and, everyone hopes, the development of a self-renewing ethos. Our description is largely taken from Emily's book on action research (Calhoun, 1994), modified by the experiences we and others have shared over the last dozen years. For many years Bruce employed "study groups" and "peer coaching" to deepen study and increase implementation and the study of student effects. Recently we have collaborated on "whole district" projects as described in Chapter 7.

Schoolwide action research is a formal way of saying, "Let's study what's happening at our school, decide if we can make it a better place by changing what and how we teach and how we relate to students and the community, study the effects, and then begin again." It is a "rolling" (Huberman, 1992) rather than a "lock-step" model for changing the workplace. Although the model has phases, they overlap, and backtracking to a prior one is common.

Although the model rolls forward and backward through its phases, it is not casual when it comes to the use of data. As we note throughout the book, our professional knowledge is not only from formal study. Each of us carries around knowledge from our own observations, and we develop knowledge with our closest colleagues as we share perceptions. The personal/social levels of knowledge are essential and invaluable. But that invaluable knowledge also tends to confirm our present practice and the progress of our students. In action research we test and expand our knowledge, and we expect to challenge ourselves and our perceptions and revise and go beyond them. We study our students and how they are responding to our teaching. We anticipate that we will find some areas where we need both to revise our conceptions and exceed them by experimenting with fresh ways of teaching and new curricular content. We discipline ourselves to expose our beliefs to examination by collecting data and studying research by others. The discipline in the inquiry is not just to learn ways of studying teaching and learning but to confront ourselves deliberately with information and ideas we did not start with. We challenge ourselves and deal with our new ideas head-on.

The Action Research Cycle

Essential is a continuous confrontation with data on the health of our school community. We move through five phases of inquiry:

1. We select an area or problem of collective interest.

2. We collect data related to this area.

3. We organize those data.

4. We interpret the data and add to it by examining related literature.

5. We take action based on this information (Calhoun & Glickman, 1993; Glickman, 1990).

These phases inherently overlap, and action researchers constantly retrace their steps and revise earlier phases before (or while) going forward again. This collective inquiry into our work (teaching) and its effects on students (learning and development) is a cyclic process and can serve as formative evaluation of initiatives we undertake as a school community.

The primary focus here is on studying what's happening to students, but we can use action research *subject* to study and improve what's happening to adults in our learning community and to study the relationship of the school to the neighborhood. Our study can be large-scale, using data from several years from our schools and some-times from others, and look at the cumulative effects of schooling. Or the scale can be small, such as looking at the immediate academic and social effects of the new social studies curriculum on students.

Of course, schoolwide action research is no panacea. It offers no magic potion to give us automatic, painless school improvement. And the process cannot be conducted by persons external to the school. The school is where renewal happens, and the process begins with ourselves. We are the ones to reform first. Our professional role is not to "fix society." We cannot change the home environment of many of our children, nor can we immediately improve the socioeco-nomic status of the families who depend on us to provide an educa-tion for their children. What we can do immediately is to make better choices about how we spend student and adult time and energy in our schools.

The idea to develop the school as a center of inquiry (Schaefer, 1967) is simple, yet its implementation requires a will beyond what is usually demanded of us. Essentially, school renewal—and the action research needed to guide school renewal—is propelled by will. The Nike slogan, "Just do it!" seems to capture the essence that distin-guishes the schools that achieve their instructional goals from those that become mired in an endless process of planning or endure long hours of labor without any effects on students' social or academic achievement (Corey, 1953; Schaefer, 1967; Sirotnik, 1987).

The quest for school renewal through action research . . .

- is a route to immediate student outcomes;
- can develop the school as a learning community;
- can build organizational capacity to solve problems;
- is a staff development program through the study of literature and on-site data and the determination of optimum actions for implementation; and
- can embrace personal and professional development.

That these goals are feasible is supported by Calhoun and her col-leagues' study of 60 schools (Calhoun & Glickman, 1993). Sites where the principal and an elected team of teacher-leaders were organized but limited amounts of technical support were provided made good progress in changing school structures (e.g., block scheduling, addi-tional tutoring for students, changes in length of course offerings), in changing the interactions among teachers and teachers and adminis-trators to more collaboration and improved communication, and even in gathering data about their focus areas. Again, though, we reiterate that direct changes in student learning depend on reaching a level where curriculum and instruction are improved. Only where intensive technical support was provided did student learning improve substantially. And in all those situations where student learning was improved, the entire faculty was involved in collective study (Calhoun & Glickman, 1993; see also, Myers, 1985; Oja & Smulyan, 1989; Rogers, Haven-O'Donnell, Hebdon, & Ferrell, 1990; Strickland, 1988).

Collaborative, Small-Group Action Research

The difference between the small-group variety and action research with larger groups is simply that fewer people are involved (sometimes only three or four from a given school), and, therefore, the impact of possible change is more restricted. However, the restriction on breadth of effect does not imply that collaborative action research is less rigorous. Two or three teachers, carefully studying the effects of instruction, involving students in assessing progress, and expanding their curricular and instructional repertoires, can affect the learning of many students and several colleagues. And, sometimes, they can become a base of strength for future, broader efforts.

Small-group action research can be focused on problems and changes in a few classrooms within a school or district or across schools and districts. The size of the action research team may be as few as two people, or it may include several teachers and administrators working with one or more staff members from a university or other external agency. These collaborative action researchers might tackle a problem they share across their classrooms, they might focus on only one classroom, or they might tackle a districtwide problem. They follow the same investigative/reflective cycle that the individual teacher-researcher follows.

Charters, Small Groups,
Voluntarism, and Open-Endedness

Action research by small, voluntary groups does not require a charter that binds the entire faculty, although the process of inquiry is otherwise virtually identical to that in a larger group, and most groups will need technical assistance. However, when an *entire* staff of a school is divided into groups whose members are to share their skills and perhaps develop action research skills or study models of teaching new to them, *then* a charter is needed to develop an agreement about full participation. The staffers are not committing to the inquiry process or to study new models of curriculum or teaching, but they *are* committing to be an active member of a little community of learners.

States of Growth: People and the Collaborative/Cooperative Models

Once again we have to think about individual differences as we consider participation in the group of models that emphasize collaborative inquiry.

Every school staff has members in every state of growth. The responses of persons in each state are fairly consistent with respect to the variety of approaches.

> *Gourmet omnivores and active consumers*—These are the important "solid citizens" of the schoolwide action research model. They are cheerful, enjoy learning, tolerate ambiguity well, and are helpful in bringing together information from various sources. They do well in small-group action research and professional learning communities or study groups, but not if a group gets bogged down. That said, however, gourmet omnivores are not necessarily candidates for leadership. Some are; some are not. But they accept leadership well.

> *Passive consumers*—These participants depend on good leadership. In vigorous action research communities, they become more active. Picking good steering committees and leadership groups is important in general, but especially important to them. In the voluntary/small-group format, they are not likely to join a group unless the school leadership actively encourages them.

> *Reticent consumers*—These people are likely to take a backseat when they can. In the volunteer formats, they usually do not volunteer. When they do, they can be destructive of the group process. In the format described above, where a strong and forthcoming principal works actively and builds strong teacher leadership, they still tend to keep to that backseat.

Critical Issues and Considerations

How valid are the theses underlying the cooperative models? Variance in success may be a product of the gritty process of making things happen. Can a really fine implementation of a well-designed model affect feelings, bring about a quality process, generate a good implementation, and offer the possibility of fine student learning? Can an OK implementation generate just modest changes but with nothing of importance happening?

Because groups can select their own directions, evaluation of cooperative models is very complicated. Essentially, studies of the effects of cooperative groups need to be done on a case-by-case basis. If we study 100 groups and find that teachers expanded their repertoires in all cases, we can conclude 100 percent efficiency. If that happened in 80 percent of the cases, we can try to learn how the others might have been more successful. Where teachers added repertoire, we can proceed to try to learn whether there were effects on students.

Clean, clear, definitive evidence about the magnitude of effects from the collaborative models is not available, but we are not operating in a vacuum either. As we have said, among the cooperative learning and collaborative models—as throughout all the staff development literature—programmatic research is rare. But there are three sources of relevant evidence. One is directly related to staff development and comes from research over 20 years that we and our colleagues have done on peer coaching and study groups and on the influence of states of growth and conceptual level on behavior in collaborative groups. We borrow a second type from the abundant research on cooperative learning with school students. That is a rich field, and much of it is directly applicable to work with adults. The third type is from studies by Emily and her colleagues (and other action research scholars) on action research. In Chapter 7 we will discuss the likelihood that the cooperative/collaborative approaches will have positive effects.

All of the collaborative models can get us somewhere—it is a question of what objectives have the most priority. Well-designed and well-implemented models will get you where you want to go because of the ability of the educators. The issue for planners is . . . where are your priorities?

Organizational Complexity

We need to consider how organizational context affects effectiveness. For example, if someone within a school makes an overture to the staff to develop a collaborative mode, is that person legitimate? If so, can he or she communicate adequately to the folks who need to be involved? Generate the resources needed? And on and on. In other words, a promising practice has to run a gamut of potential obstacles to be implemented well.

But . . . the important movement toward collaborative study groups and professional learning communities runs into the norms of schools in a serious way. We strongly recommend that the first step in establishing them is to develop a charter that generates a different normative situation. The problem is less one of procedure than one of culture. A charter won't settle all the issues or the behavior of the entire group, but—as we indicated in Chapter 3—we don't want a situation where coaches or mentors have to climb a high cultural mountain to pursue their work, which is inevitably delicate. Nor do we want the development of learning communities to run a gamut of social system–related obstacles.

It would be a shame if intended professional learning communities ended up just being extensions of the periodic grade- and department-level meetings we have had for what seems forever or the monthly one-hour general faculty meetings that inevitably have to be occupied with logistics. The examples given by some serious advocates are just that. Real inquiry goes far beyond the exchanges of information and descriptions of practice that have been typical in the grade-level or department meetings.

Participation and Effects

Clearly the approaches that rely on a single small group within a staff or even two small volunteer groups will not, however well implemented, reach a large portion of the students in a school. However, they may have a fine positive effect on those educators who participate in them and the children they teach. And, when most of the staff are involved but not in coordination with one another, the resulting initiatives will probably not work together and will have weak schoolwide cumulative effects—these will not get us very far. Effective professional development of any kind is demanding. And the collaborative models require considerable energy. You can't just organize a staff into groups and hope for effects. You have to work hard to develop productive learning communities.

5

Curricular and Instructional Initiatives

Schools, Districts, and States

There is solid evidence that 21st-century skills and knowledge can be taught effectively. The core of those skills is intelligent behavior. Therefore, aspects of intelligence are included in the legitimate and reachable goals of curriculum.

—our reflective observer

What happens if you believe that a major curriculum area needs attention? What kinds of professional development should be organized?

There are no yellow brick roads to easy change in curriculum and teaching. There *are* a series of tasks to be followed to increase the likelihood that productive change will take place and student learning will be enriched as a consequence.

1. A promising curriculum needs to be developed or selected. It can be new or old, but it is new to the schools that will use it. That curriculum contains new or improved types of content and good ways of teaching it.

2. Appropriate professional development needs to be designed, including follow-up. We advocate the theory-demonstration-practice-peer coaching format (see the "Training Paradigm" section later in this chapter), with participants organized into teams and workshops interspersed with peer meetings. A cadre of "trainers" needs to be developed, and implementation support from administrators, district staff, consultants, and cadre is essential.

3. Estimates need to be made of the amount of time to schedule for that professional development—the workshops and follow-up peer coaching and support—*and* that time has to be arranged. We operate on the premise that, in a major curriculum area, a change of about one-quarter of the curriculum (larger changes are extremely rare) would require about ten half-day workshops plus time for peer study.

4. The embedded study of implementation guides support efforts.

5. The embedded study of student learning by teachers and cadre and organizers provides data for participants and organizers to assess progress. (See "Kindergarten Goes to School" below.)

6. Periodic formal summative assessment is also embedded, preferably with performance measures administered by a trained team and analyzed by the initiative coordinators. Results are fed to all stakeholders: students, parents, teachers, administrators, and policymakers.

7. The sixth task leads to taking stock and making changes in the initiative as indicated by the evidence.

No exotic processes ensure curriculum improvement—just straightforward work through these logical tasks.

Initiatives to improve schools can be made by individuals, study groups, school faculties, clusters of schools, districts, or states. A district or state can prepare coaches to be a major part of a large-scale initiative, but unless they offer workshops rather than offering training to individuals and small groups, the costs would be very large.

Building on Success

Some very successful initiatives have changed curriculum or instruction with fine results in the core subjects. Enough is known that successful models can be described and used. And the successes contrast sharply with a host of failed initiatives that employed ineffective models.

Content—curriculum and instruction in the curriculum areas—gives definition to this type of staff development. Various professional development processes can be employed, but improving curriculum and instruction of small and large magnitudes is the target. Curriculum reform has a long history; studies were most dense during the period of the academic reform movement (1955–1980) (see Joyce, Calhoun, & Hopkins, 1999), when foundations and government agencies like the National Science Foundation funded efforts to update curriculums in the academic areas.

Success for All

For more than 20 years, this literacy curriculum has generated consistent if moderate gains with the most unlikely populations of Title I students. The magnitude of its success is dramatized by the title of the book summarizing the approach and its successes: *2 Million Children* (Slavin, Madden, Chambers, & Haxby, 2009). Success for All asks that schools vote to participate, works within the confines of the usually available time for staff development, and provides facilitators to follow up on the training and help schools adjust as they implement the curriculum materials that are provided. Effect sizes for a year range between 0.30 and 0.40. Some students gain more in comparison with those in schools not using Success for All. The effort is important for a number of reasons, including that schools in economically poor areas were targeted, and the results conflict sharply with the dismal findings from less-structured Title I efforts.

Reading Recovery

Reading Recovery is a program for struggling readers in the first grade. Specially trained tutors work one-on-one for 30 minutes a day for 12 to 20 weeks. Evaluating the effects is complex, but we estimate that the program effectively reaches about three-quarters of the students referred to it, and the effects apparently persist through elementary school and beyond (see, for example, Pinnell, Lyone, Deford, Bryk, & Seltzer, 1994; Swartz & Klein, 1997).

Steady Improvement of Biology Curriculums

Biological Sciences Curriculum Study (BSCS) was developed 40 years ago (Schwab, 1965) and is still going strong, with communication among teachers facilitated through the Eisenhower Program and the dot-com environment of today. The program is designed to teach the process of science through units in which the students are led through experiments to test or generate knowledge in biology. The instructor ideally has an ongoing study of his or her own going in the classroom and shares progress with the students. BSCS conducted (and still conducts) internal evaluations that have shown that it achieves its goals.

The durability of BSCS is probably due to its focus on teachers who have much in common—they staff the biology and general science courses in our schools. The manuals and textbooks are designed for the self-training of those instructors, and summer workshops and other experiences are designed with the theory-demonstration-practice paradigm that appears to be so effective in helping teachers develop complex skills. The efforts and writings of the late Susan Loucks-Horsley were important in the BSCS movement. The influence of the academic reform movement and research on professional development are combined in many of her books (see, especially, her description in Loucks-Horsley, Stiles, Mundry, Love, & Hewson, 2010).

Over the years, other inquiry-oriented science and social studies curriculums have generated fine student effects (see Bredderman, 1983; El-Nemr, 1979) in content, scientific method, and positive attitudes toward the content. Analytic approaches to the teaching of writing have done very well (see Hillocks, 1987). The curriculum models range from very direct ones with specifically defined content and procedures to cooperative learning models and nondirective teaching.

Let's look at the development of procedures that permit teachers to learn new repertoire, which is critical if changes in curriculum are to take place. Actually, this kind of training research focuses on the study of how educators learn.

The Training Paradigm

Twenty-five years ago a serious problem in staff development was the implementation of its content. When universities and central offices offered training in curriculum and instruction, few researchers studied implementation. In other words, if teachers took a course in, say, the study of arithmetic, there was rarely follow-up, including the collection of data, to find out if anyone used the content of the course, let alone whether student learning changed or increased. However, as the venue of staff development shifted to the school district, which had a real interest in whether a curricular or instructional change was made, the study of training elements and their effects became more urgent and prominent.

The following description is from our own work and experience over the last 30 years.

To use a new curriculum pattern or model of teaching, several types of learning are needed.

- Knowledge is terribly important. Teachers and administrators cannot implement a new curriculum without the knowledge that supports it and is available in their minds as courses, units, and lessons are prepared and used.
- Skill in planning is the key to implementation as the curriculum is introduced to the students. New teaching moves (skills) may also be needed.
- Preparation for use in the classroom is another essential.

Thus, the training needs to provide knowledge, skill, and preparation for implementation.

Several training elements are combined to generate the requisite learning:

- *Demonstrations* are a critical element. Organizers frequently underestimate the number needed. In our work, 20 or more spread over a year are not unusual. Most are taped lessons and units with students.
- *Presentations*—readings, lecture/discussions, and the analysis of curriculum materials—are interwoven with the demonstrations.
- *Preparation* for implementation is vital and, again, interwoven with demonstrations, readings, and presentations. Teachers need to reach the classroom with lessons in hand, complete with the materials they will use.
- *Implementation* is conducted as an inquiry, and the teachers are prepared to study student learning *from the beginning*. In a literacy curriculum in the primary grades (K–2), the acquisition of sight vocabulary is studied, word by word. Acquisition of alphabet recognition is tracked. Numbers of books read by each student are reported. A "log" guides the teachers through these studies and into questions for the trainers as the year progresses.

These elements occur in sessions spread over several months or even a school year. A few days at the beginning followed by one-day or half-day sessions every three or four weeks is often about right.

Well-organized and delivered training can generate knowledge and skill and preparation for short-term implementation. Yet long-term implementation usually does not occur—only about 10 percent of the teachers master the new model and incorporate it into their repertoire. In a long series of studies, a variety of remedies were explored. In the short run, a very successful remedy was to have the trainers follow the teachers and administrators into their classrooms, discuss implementation, and help them with the stickiest items. The rate of implementation rose to over 90 percent. Great, but costly. Speaking practically, sending the trainers to provide the "follow-up" is a *very* expensive option, as is training coaches to follow up. So, borrowing from studies on therapies for mild neuroses where the clients did quite well when organized into self-help groups, we organized the teachers into peer-coaching groups who met together, discussed their teaching, and, in the best circumstances, planned lessons that they both tried and then discussed with one another. Well, the implementation rate went up to 90 percent with the teachers supporting themselves.

Thus, at present in our work, participants are organized into peer-coaching teams of two or three that meet regularly to plan lessons and discuss progress. In the "follow-up" sessions, progress is shared. Alternatively, teams of teachers from schools are brought together for sharing and "booster" training and work in their schools to achieve implementation (for a general discussion of the development and researching of the "training model," see Joyce & Showers, 2002).

In other words, it turned out that there was nothing wrong with the teachers' learning capacity. If the environment was arranged correctly, the teachers could learn new curricular and instructional patterns, build them into their repertoire, and then use them as they thought right for years on end. The tough part was the move into serious implementation, when they needed each other and could help each other get through the invisible barrier that had been the obstacle.

The important outcome of the long series of studies was that new curriculums and models of teaching were well within the reach of teachers and administrators—*provided* that the staff development was arranged correctly (see Figure 5.1).

Training and the Content of Training

Virtually all educators can learn and implement models of teaching and curriculum, provided the environment is designed so that they

Figure 5.1			
Training Element	Effects on Knowledge	Effects on Short-Term Use (% of Participants)	Effects on Long-Term Use (% of Participants)
Study of Rationale (Readings, Discussions, Lectures)	Very Positive	5–10%	5–10%
Rationale Plus Demonstrations (10 or more)	Very Positive	5–20%	5–10%
Rationale Plus Demonstrations Plus Planning of Units and Lessons	Very Positive	80–90%	5–10%
All the Above, Plus Peer Coaching	Very Positive	90%+	90%+

can study the rationale; see a good many demonstrations; plan units and lessons for the students they teach; and study the responses of those students, including what they learn and at what rate. However, the curricular and instructional content needs to be good—something that will enable students to learn new things or learn old things better. Good training does not rehabilitate poor curriculum. Good content does not get implemented without good opportunities to learn it.

Commitment and Competence

Huberman and Miles (1984) extracted from their extensive study the proposition that "commitment follows competence." They argued that teachers moved from a position of initial skepticism to a position of pragmatic acceptance of practices that were new to them as they became more competent in the use of those practices. The implication for staff development organizers is to put less energy into trying to persuade teachers that they will like a new practice and more energy into helping those practitioners master the new strategies. Trainers whose content is models of teaching and curriculum new to their clients can expect an initial "push-back" that will lessen as the new content becomes a part of the teaching repertoire. Or teachers may initially push away the content or some of it because they don't believe it will fill the bill. As they get good at the new repertoire, they often reevaluate their initial reaction.

Large-Scale Programs: A 2008–2009 Iowa Initiative in Literacy

We draw again on our own work for an illustration of a very large program where local personnel were prepared to "cotrain" with the expert consultant and provide support to teachers and administrators across the entire state of Iowa. The State Department of Education made the initiative in literacy. The centerpiece of this literacy initiative is training in a central location for 500 teachers, principals, central office staff, and area educational agency consultants working in or with over 50 schools. Emily is the primary consultant and trainer, and her literacy model of teaching, the Picture Word Inductive Model (see Joyce, Weil, & Calhoun, 2009), is the content focus. The intent is to help teachers and principals study literacy; work to strengthen the teaching of alphabet recognition, sight vocabulary, and writing; expand the use of inductive and inquiry lessons and student skill in inductive thinking and inquiry; and help students learn how to build vocabulary and reading skills—while also implementing the new Iowa Core Curriculum. The long-term and immediate goals are to accelerate students' literacy development *and* their learning capacity.

This professional development opportunity is organized by the Iowa Department of Education (IDE) and supported in schools by Iowa's Area Education Agencies (AEAs). AEA consultants work with school teams and district office staff to support the study of student performance and the implementation of instructional strategies and curriculum. In June of 2008, school teams—including principals—gathered in Des Moines for three days of "start-up" training. Carlene Lodermeier, literacy consultant for the Iowa Department of Education and the primary organizer; Emily, the lead trainer; and ten other educators—five teachers, three AEA consultants, and two current/former IDE consultants—facilitated this initial work, as well as the four follow-up days of professional development scheduled between October 2008 and June 2009. All except one of these 12 persons had experience in using the Picture Word Inductive Model (PWIM) in schools.

The basic theory-demonstration-practice model is used during these collective professional development sessions. As part of follow-up, the principals and teachers work together between sessions in a "peer-coaching" framework, helping one another implement PWIM and study the effects on student learning. Throughout the year, teachers and administrators send Carlene the results of their study of student learning and reflections on their use of PWIM—including problems needing attention. Emily and the Facilitation Team study these data and use this information in planning sessions and to select content for other avenues of support.

Both Carlene and Emily consider this seven days of face-to-face professional development "light support" in relation to what teachers and administrators are being asked to do:

1. carry on disciplined action research on how students are progressing in learning the alphabet, developing sight words and vocabulary, and writing informative prose;

2. carry on disciplined action research into their current instructional practice and on the implementation of new instructional practices and curriculum;

3. use student data to design lessons as they implement the Picture Word Inductive Model; and

4. collaboratively study student performance, plan lessons, and solve problems.

Several types of support were included in the design of the initiative. Carlene developed an application form that included "Expectations for Participation" for school team members and district staff to review prior to their commitment and an "Assurances" form that asked principals and superintendents to initial their understanding of the conditions of participation. Principals and district office staff were asked to schedule time for collaborative work by school teams in their buildings throughout the school year (built in to the school calendar). They were asked to schedule ongoing support from their AEA consultant and/or literacy strategist. Principals were asked to coplan and teach PWIM lessons on a regular basis and to participate in collaborative meetings regarding student data and the study of implementation. The 56 school teams that were accepted each received $5,000 from the state to defray a portion of the costs of stipends for the days during the summer and for travel, lodging, and materials.

Another avenue of support was the Statewide Reading Team (SWRT). Carlene, with the support of her supervisor Jim Reese and other IDE officials and the AEA regional directors, has worked for over ten years to build a strong base of support for schools working to improve literacy. The Statewide Reading Team—comprising primarily regional intermediate service consultants, district office staff from large school districts, and some high-implementing teachers and principals—is a central component of this base. Members of this group help organize the data from schools, work to identify and resolve problems, and, through Carlene, work with the PWIM Facilitation Team to provide additional support to schools. SWRT, which meets about ten days a year, also identified aspects of instructional and curricular content that they needed more assistance with to provide optimum support in schools and built this content into some of their meeting days.

And, while there were and are many other actions that individual teachers, administrators, and consultants provide (such as coaching via e-mail, sharing lessons across schools), there are two other initiativewide mechanisms for supporting the professional development of individuals and the group as a whole: (1) easy access to all materials via an IDE Web site and DVDs and (2) the Iowa Communications Network (ICN) interactive broadcasts. The Every Child Reads (ECR) Web site is sponsored by the Iowa Department of Education. It serves many purposes. Any participant in this initiative can go online and download materials shared at any session and access links to other curriculum and instructional materials available from the state and other sources. Also, all participants are given DVDs with teacher demonstrations of the instructional strategies for use at home and with their collaboration teams. Five ICN interactive broadcasts were scheduled across the year to provide opportunities for questions, support in using student data, additional demonstrations, and curriculum and assessment content.

We think of this effort as a collective support model, where the professional development organized by the state department of education reaches teachers and principals in many schools. There is staff development time away from the schools, with participants benefiting from different perspectives and a larger professional community, and within each school. Individual and collective action research is supported in every school. Enough staff development and on-site support is provided to enable teachers to begin to implement the Picture Word Inductive Model in their classrooms and to work with peers as they study their practice and its effects on student learning. The model is well backed by research, including tests with hundreds of elementary school children, K–5, and older struggling readers (see, for example, Joyce, Calhoun, Jutras, & Newlove, 2006).

The state is an appropriate-sized organization to provide support to this number of teachers, and the regional agencies see themselves as part of the organization necessary to successfully supporting something of this magnitude. Each district and/or school has to budget to enable the teachers to travel and have time and resources for working together. Although the state provides an offset against these expenses, the districts and schools have to make a contribution. From the teachers, the contribution is energy and time and the determination to add to their repertoire an approach to teaching that will enhance student learning. For administrators, it is the many actions that make up active instructional leadership—such as participating in meetings, working with and helping teachers use data, coplanning lessons, making regular collaborative time available, and monitoring and supporting implementation.

We hear rumors that organizations the size of the state Department of Education are too distanced from districts and schools to provide meaningful support, but that is simply an erroneous impression. The question is whether they are willing to identify an area of need—clearly a good many Iowa teachers are interested in learning to teach literacy more effectively, and the state can provide service on a large scale—and marshal resources from multiple sources to pursue commonly valued goals.

We are going to occupy much of the rest of this chapter with a study of a literacy program built around the Picture Word Inductive Model (Calhoun, 1999), because it illustrates a complete package of curriculum change from initial assessment to development and, thence, to training and follow-up and the study of student learning. Again, professional development is central, but in school improvement initiatives the development of the curriculum itself is important, and evaluation instruments have to be tailored to the initiative.

Kindergarten Goes to School in the Northern Lights School Division

In the following pages we report an example from our collaboration with school district administrators and teachers in Alberta, Canada. A serious need for curriculum and instructional improvement was identified. An initiative was generated and studied with curriculum development and professional development working together. The investment in days customarily allotted to professional development was enlarged considerably. An unusual aspect of the evaluation is that it had to address an important cross-national and provincial controversial issue about reading in kindergarten. In addition, issues involving gender, ethnicity, and learning disabilities had to be addressed in the evaluation. One or more of those issues usually need to be addressed in the study of any professional development or school improvement issue using any model.

The study was originally reported in a paper presented to the Asian/Pacific Educational Research Association—"The Tending of Diversity Through a Robust Core Literacy Curriculum: Gender, Socioeconomic Status, Learning Disabilities, and Ethnicity" (Joyce, Calhoun, Hrycauk, & Hrycauk, 2006).

Working with us in the study and the preparation of the report were Marilyn Hrycauk, The Northern Lights School Division #69, Bonnyville, Alberta, Canada, and Walter Hrycauk, chair of the board of trustees, The Northern Lights School Division, Bonnyville, Alberta, Canada.

First, a note on Northern Lights School Division #69:

The division is in northern Alberta and spans over 200 kilometers with a geographic area of 14,800 square kilometers. Schools are located in the major towns of Cold Lake, Bonnyville, and Lac La Biche (each has a population of about 6,000), the villages of Glendon and Plamondon; the hamlet of Casden; and the rural areas of Ardmore, Iron River, and Wandering river. The division operates a school on 4 Wing, a major air force installation near Cold Lake. There are about 6,000 students. The genders are about even in number. Students with mild to moderate learning disabilities compose about 11 percent of the student population, and about 8 percent are of interest here, because the diagnosed disabilities theoretically affect learning to read and write. Students whose parents identify them as aboriginal make up 28 percent of the population (1,675 students). Of these, 230 are First Nations persons who live on reservations and have "status rights," including the rights to treaty benefits and to inherit land. Sixty-two are First Nations students who do not live on reservations and do not have status rights. Metis students make up the majority. They have some aboriginal ancestors. The 976 Metis students are 16 percent of the district student population. There is one Inuit student—origins are in the arctic areas of North America.

You probably noticed that the logistics in Northern Lights are daunting. The area is close to the size of Connecticut, yet vans shuttle back and forth taking people to face-to-face meetings and workshops. Telephone, fax, and e-mail are integral to communication, and as this is written, fine interactive television meeting rooms have been developed.

Historically, student achievement can be described as Canadian/U.S. normal. The Canadian distribution of student achievement is about the same as the U.S. distribution, as reported in the National Assessment of Educational Progress studies (see Donahue, 1999). However, by high school, Canadian achievement in mathematics and science is substantially above U.S. figures (see OECD, 2007).

Until the new curriculum was implemented, "standard" test results had been relentlessly average. About two-thirds of the students appeared to learn to read adequately or better. About 30 percent of the students did not learn to read or write well. Males, students with learning disabilities, and aboriginal students all lagged in comparison to their counterparts. The provincial government generated curriculum changes regularly with little effect on student learning, including variance due to demographic differences. A very large provincial investment in special education had little effect.

Rationales: Meeting Diverse Needs Through Literacy in Kindergarten

As we indicated just above, curriculum and its evaluation needed to address both the needs of diverse populations and the serious issue about the appropriateness of teaching reading in kindergarten.

Approaches to Tending Diverse Student Populations

Generally, there are three approaches to meeting the needs of diverse student populations.

1. The first emphasizes inclusion—ensuring that various types of students are not deprived of full participation in the mainstream schooling process and that equity in educational opportunity is achieved.

2. The second emphasizes the development of program variations to support the development of students with ethnic, socioeconomic, or social/psychological characteristics that are different from those of the "mainstream" population. In the United States, the massive Title I and special education initiatives generally take this approach.

3. The third, the one discussed and reported here, builds on current research on the teaching of literacy and emphasizes the development of a robust core curriculum that has room for the development of the talents of nearly all students.

We have no intention of pitting the three approaches against one another.

Inclusion is important. Many natural forces separate students from one another. Prominently, differences in demography among neighborhoods can generate inequalities related to SES and ethnic differences, differences that can have a lifelong effect. As difficult as it is, we need to seek ways to reduce the effects of de facto segregation and other forces that generate exclusion and inequality.

Targeted initiatives are important. We need to continue the search for ways of helping students whose characteristics make them candidates for low academic, social, and personal achievement. Efforts of developers, like the SIM group at the University of Kansas, are vital (Deshler & Schumaker, 2006). They are particularly so because large-scale initiatives to target students hampered by low socioeconomic environments have, on the whole, been very unsuccessful, as have many programs that serve students with mild or moderate learning disabilities. Gender can be very important in the literacy areas. In many school districts, males lag seriously behind females from primary levels through high school and, in the United States, college, where 60 percent of enrolled students are females who, once there, outperform males on average (see, for example, Brooks, 2005).

In Northern Lights, we combined inclusion with major curriculum change, beginning in kindergarten but continuing in the primary grades and combined with a program to reach struggling readers in the upper grades and secondary schools. Here we focus on the kindergarten initiative. The evaluation was designed so that the effects on the various populations described above could be examined.

Issues in Kindergarten Education

We turn now to the curriculum and its theoretical base. The evaluation study tests the theory that most kindergarten children are ready to learn to read and that doing so has long-lasting effects. In other words, this initiative has theoretical practical implications for the field of early childhood education. The question is

> Can we, using the Picture Word Inductive Model (see Calhoun, 1999), teach kindergarten children to read—and what are the implications for the controversy about whether formal literacy instruction is good for young children?

Kindergarten has been an interesting area. A substantial movement has worked hard against the formal teaching of reading in kindergarten (Elkind, 1987, 2001) on the grounds that it is not "developmentally appropriate." On the other hand, innovations in the teaching of literacy have developed curricular and instructional models that have substantial promise to teach young children to learn to read in the early years. To educators and laypeople alike, the term *developmentally appropriate* makes intuitive sense. Everyone would hope that schooling would make contact with the student's developmental level. However, the position papers of national organizations state clearly that reading is *not* "developmentally appropriate" (IRA, 1998; IRA & NAEYC, 1998). Some experts even question whether having "full day" kindergarten is too much, let alone a curriculum in reading (Natale, 2001).

The title of an April 2005 article in the *San Diego Union-Tribune*, "Kindergarten or 'Kindergrind'" (Gao, 2005) captures the controversy. Opponents of formal study of reading claimed that teaching reading was necessarily a move toward a harsh and rote curriculum that did not meet the needs of the children. The government agencies responsible for Reading First and No Child Left Behind took the "developmentally inappropriate" stance toward kindergarten. Certainly they did not promote reading below first grade, even as they promoted phonemic awareness for K–1 students.

The views expressed by the national organizations and government panels are not shared by all "experts" on reading.

Years ago, one of the most respected scholars of early reading in the United States presented an extensive argument (Durkin, 1966) for beginning early, and her rationale is essentially unquestioned by other scholars. In a longitudinal study, Hanson and Farrell (1995) found that the effects of a reading curriculum in kindergarten could be seen in the academic achievement of 12th-grade students. Finally, the "father" of the idea of kindergarten, Fredrich Froebel, emphasized the need for a rich environment that would pull students into inquiry and development: neither a free-play school in a play-only environment nor a rough-edged curriculum.

From our perspective, the real issue is whether a comprehensive reading curriculum can be developmentally appropriate, meaning can the children learn to read and do so without harm.

The complexity for Northern Lights and us was that we not only needed to work together to build a curriculum, generate the staff development to implement it, and modify it depending on the teachers' experience with it, but the evaluation needed to deal with the early childhood curricular controversy *and* the effect on a diverse population. It is worth noting that many curriculum innovations are attended by similar concerns. For example, when mathematics and science curriculums are taught with inductive methods, questions are raised about whether "basic" information and computation will suffer. Evaluations need to include the study of effects on diverse populations and deal with the important issues attendant to a curriculum change in any area.

Curriculum Design

Important for our early literacy curriculum was the emergence of the Picture Word Inductive Model from the tradition of the language experience frame of reference with the addition of concept formation and attainment models of teaching

(Calhoun, 1999). The Picture Word Inductive Model designs cycles that begin with photographs of scenes whose content is within the ability of the students to describe. For example, photographs can be of aspects of the local community, or they can take students around the world with photos of scenes they can relate to—a picture of a scene in an outdoor market is an example. The students take turns identifying objects and actions in the picture. The teacher spells the words, drawing lines from the words to the elements in the picture to which they refer, creating a picture dictionary. The students are given copies of the words, and they identify them using the picture dictionary. They proceed to classify the words using the well-tested inductive model of learning, noting their similarities and differences. The teacher selects some of their categories for extended study. Both phonetic features and structural characteristics are studied. The teacher models the creation of titles and sentences, and the students create same, dictating them and learning to read them. The students gradually learn to assemble titles and sentences into paragraphs about the content of the picture. The picture word cycles (inquiries into the pictures) generally take from three to five weeks.

A central assumption is that students need to become inquirers into language, seeking to build their sight vocabularies and studying the characteristics of those words, trying to build generalizations about phonetic and structural characteristics.

We imagined an environment where students would progress from their developed listening/speaking vocabularies to the reading of words, sentences, and longer text that they had created, where they would examine simple books in a relaxed atmosphere, where they would begin to write with scribbling and simple illustrations, where they would be read to regularly, and where comprehension strategies would be modeled for them through the reading and study of charming fiction and nonfiction books. If the work of childhood is play, we imagined the students playfully working their way into literacy. Froebel envisioned capitalizing on children's natural propensity for play to enable them to mature socially and cognitively by engaging in increasingly complex activities. We wished to create an environment where students would learn to read in a joyful fashion.

Professional Development, Implementation, and Student Learning

At the beginning of the school year, the start of kindergarten was delayed for a week after Grades 1 through 12 began. This week was used to introduce the kindergarten teachers to the curriculum for teaching reading (none had taught reading formally in their past). The training model described above was used to design the sessions and the follow-up.

School principals, central office personnel, and a cadre of teachers attended the sessions and experienced additional days of support because they, and the primary consultant-trainer, became a Literacy Team whose members visited the teachers and offered advice and support through the school years. Kindergarten teams from the schools became peer-coaching teams. In addition, designated staff development days were augmented, and a day's session was organized for seven occasions during each school year. Prior to those sessions, the teachers filled out logs reporting implementation and identifying problems to be solved. And they studied the acquisition of alphabet recognition and vocabulary through the year and reported progress in the logs. The resulting information was used not only by the teachers but also by the consultants and literacy cadre as they planned and organized the follow-up training sessions.

Also, the literacy team tested the kindergarten children using the Gunning Procedure, described below, and the children in first through seventh grade using the Gray Oral Reading Test. Altogether, the literacy team participated in the design of the curriculum and the nature of the professional development, provided training including visitation support, and evaluated implementation and effects on students.

Results I: Implementation

The study of implementation was accomplished through a combination of self-report logs and observations conducted by consultants and central office personnel.

All the teachers implemented the curriculum with a good deal of enthusiasm. They were particularly buoyed by watching the students acquire alphabet recognition and sight vocabulary and observing them as they read sentences, paragraphs, and simple books. And, as some of the students moved rapidly to about the level of good average second-grade readers, the teachers reported considerable satisfaction. A member of one team summarized their beliefs: "We were sure these kids couldn't learn to read. Then they did. We think we can teach any little kid who comes to school how to read and read well." Here you feel the "commitment follows competence" thesis coming to life.

The teachers reached varying levels of skill with aspects of the curriculum, but we judged that all had mastered the important skills and were employing them comfortably by the end of the first year.

Results II: Embedded Study of Alphabet and Vocabulary

The teachers measured alphabet recognition out of the context of words, using flash cards. By midyear nearly all students recognized all the letters and the others 20 or more; the latter students recognized all letters before year's end. Recognition of the words shaken out of the pictures was also assessed out of context—again with flash cards—and, by the end of each cycle, most students in each section recognized nearly all the words. By year's end, three-fourths of the students recognized *all* of the 150 or so words shaken out during the year, and no student recognized fewer than 120. (The students had learned sight recognition of a considerable number of other words as well, but the testing highlighted just those prominent in each PWIM cycle. The findings were important to the teachers—typically in the school division, only a handful of students entered first grade able to read the simplest books, and only about one-third had full recognition of the alphabet (knowledge of which is the best predictor of first-grade reading achievement).

Results III: Formal Assessment of Competence in Reading— The Gunning Procedure and the Gray Oral Reading Test

At the end of the kindergarten year, the students were administered what we call the Gunning procedure. Then, in Grades 1 through 7, the Gray Oral Reading Test was given to those who were still in the district at the end of each school year.

The study of implementation was accomplished through a combination of self-report logs and observations conducted by consultants and central office personnel.

The **Gunning procedure,** developed by Thomas Gunning (1998), presents to the students trade books that have been selected because they represent increasingly more demanding levels of reading.

Gunning Levels

Level 1: Picture Level—The vocabulary is very small, sometimes only a half dozen words, and is closely linked to pictures.

Level 2: Caption Level—There are a few more words, and there is more action— more to comprehend. Each page has a phrase that moves the book along.

Level 3: Easy Sight Level—Extended text is introduced. The student has to read text beyond what is illustrated.

Levels 4–6: Beginning Reading Levels—The vocabularies increase, the complexity of the stories increases, and the understanding of even lavishly illustrated books depends on the reading of complex text.

Level 7: Grade 2-A—These are larger, more complex books. The student who can read at this level can read a large number of books on many topics and do so independently.

The books are presented to the students, and the cover pages are discussed briefly. Then, the students read the books and answer questions designed to assess comprehension of the major aspects of the books. To ensure that the students are not familiar with the books, they are selected from titles published in Great Britain that have not yet been distributed in Canada. The Gunning assessment is of performance. The students' levels are measured directly by having them read material at various levels of complexity. Performance measures are strikingly different from multiple-choice tests, where reading levels are inferred from response to structured tasks rather than from engagement in reading books and text passages.

The Gunning Results in Kindergarten

Table 5.1 presents the results for the initial kindergarten cohort group at the end of the kindergarten year.

Table 5.1	Percent of Students Reaching Gunning Levels at End-of-Year Testing	
Level		**Percent Reaching Level**
Picture (a few words, closely connected to pictures)		2
Caption (picture books, with text in captions)		26
Easy sight (simple text that carries meaning)		30
Above Easy Sight (extended text in complex stories)		42

The students learned to read somewhat better than first-grade students usually did in our school district with an important addition—they *all* learned to read at some level. All eight sections apparently succeeded in bringing all the students to some level of print literacy. About 40 percent of the students appeared to be able to read extended text, and another 30 percent manifested emergent ability to read extended text. Twenty percent reached the 2-A level, which includes long and complex passages and requires the exercise of complex skills both to decode and infer word meanings. All the students could manage at least the simplest level of books. Very important to us was that no students experienced abject failure. Even the student who enters first grade reading independently at the picture level carries alphabet recognition, a substantial storehouse of sight words, and an array of phonetic and structural concepts to the first-grade experience. However, a half dozen students needed to be watched closely in Grade 1 because, although they were able to handle books at the caption level, they labored at the task, manifesting difficulty either in recognizing text-graphics relationships or using their phonetic or structural generalizations to attack unfamiliar words.

In previous years, about 30 percent would have been at the picture level or below at the end of Grade 1 at the end of the academic year.

Grades 5 and 7

The Gray Oral Reading Test is built around a series of passages that the students read to the assessor. The passages proceed from the simple to the complex.

The assessor studies the students' ability to recognize the words and apply strategies for recognizing the words not recognized by sight. The assessor supplies words that are not recognized after a reasonable period of time (about three seconds). After the reading of each passage, questions are asked to assess comprehension of the content. The test yields scores on fluency and comprehension that have been normed on a substantial population of students. Thus, the results here can be compared with the normative picture.

The Gray Oral Reading Test (GORT) has been administered annually to that first group of kindergarten students who have remained in the school division. At the end of fifth grade, 69 were still enrolled in division schools. At the end of fifth grade, the national GORT average Grade Level Equivalent (GLE) score in comprehension is 6.0, as is the usual average fifth-grade student's in the division. For the 69 students, the average was GLE 7.7. Contrary to the doctrine that teaching kindergarten students with a formal literacy curriculum will be damaging later, it appears that these students had not been damaged but, rather, had prospered. Importantly, only four students were below the 5.0 level, and just one of these was a struggling reader. At the end of seventh grade, the mean GLE was 10.0.

Curriculum development may have bypassed the controversies as far as kindergarten is concerned.

Diversity and the Initial Kindergarten Population

We are concerned here with gender, socioeconomic status (SES), learning disabilities, and ethnicity.

Gender

Gender did not influence levels of success from kindergarten through fifth grade. The distributions of scores for boys and girls were almost identical. For the United States as a whole, the National Center for Educational Statistics distributions for fourth grade indicate that the males are at approximately the 30th percentile of the female distribution.

SES

The distributions of scores for students having or not having subsidies for lunch were also approximately equal.

Learning Disabilities

As is typical in our division, about 28 kindergarten students were identified by special education diagnostic procedures as having special needs. By fifth grade, all but eight of those students had been discontinued from special education because they showed no signs of disabilities. In the past all 28 would have been continued.

Ethnicity

In our population area, the major concern was with the achievement of aboriginal students. In the district, nearly all the aboriginal students had done poorly. In the sample of our kindergarten students, there were eight aboriginal students. Their average comprehension score in the fifth grade was 7.0; just one was below 6.0.

Summary

As student achievement for the entire population of kindergarten students rose with the implementation of the formal and more robust curriculum in literacy, it appears that the subpopulations benefited simultaneously. As we look at the students who have just graduated from seventh grade, the females are prospering literacy-wise, and so are the males. Mild to moderate learning disabilities appear to be diminishing. SES did not inhibit growth. And, in the area where we have the skimpiest evidence, ethnicity, in this case the progress of aboriginals did not appear to suffer the dampening effect that ordinarily occurs. As this is written, the students have exited seventh grade, and the high achievement continues, with only two at the fifth- to sixth-grade norms.

Interpretation

This is a small-scale study, but we are on the side of studies where implementation and student learning are closely studied, and precision in measurement is on the side of small, careful studies. The controls are students in the past in the district—in the year before this study began, just one student entered first grade able to read at the sight level on the Gunning scale—and normative data for North American school districts.

Testing the waters of a multidimensional, humane approach to kindergarten learning, we believe there is good reason for optimism. In the next few years, the curriculum in kindergarten was implemented in 80 classes in 43 schools in another setting; this is described in Chapter 7.

What do you predict? Will moving to such large numbers enhance or reduce the effect? Or will it stay about the same?

Curricular and Instructional Improvement Through Professional Development

We included this study to try to make real the overall process when we decide to make an improvement in student learning through staff development focused on changes in curriculum or instruction. Another purpose was to unpack the simplicity and directness of the process.

Note that only measures of performance were used—we lobby unabashedly for them. The commercial multiple-choice instruments do not measure performance, and many are not validated against the goal behavior—in this case the ability to read. By the way, the scores on provincial tests, which are of the multiple-choice, brief variety, did rise in those schools, but what the rise means in terms of ability to read is not nearly as clear as it is in the case of the performance measures.

In Sum

Curriculum change is initiated when policymakers at the state, district, or school level believe either that there should be a change in *what* is taught—that new content should be introduced in one of the core curriculum areas—or the *achievement* of current content needs to be elevated. In either case, professional development will be the key to implementation at a level where the purposes of the initiative are achieved.

6

The Menus for "Professional Development" Days

A Long Road From Celebration to Condemnation to . . .

Short doesn't equate with bad. It's the quality that counts. Some of the offbeat stuff just gives me a new perspective. Some of the worst days are a good workshop on a practical skill I already have.

—our reflective observer

When the field of staff development was fermenting during the late 1960s and early 1970s, a remarkable thing happened. States gave school districts permission to apply district-offered professional development events toward recertification. Thus the SD unit was born to be used as college credits had been used before. Staff development "days" were funded and calendared. The workshop concept was transfused. And the needs assessment was invented to give teachers a voice in the content of their staff development.

Content From Teachers and Governments

The needs assessment, combined with the assignment of workdays dedicated to staff development, gave rise to smorgasbords of workshops on those days. The inclusion of teachers as such a direct influence on the content of the workshops was much celebrated by teachers' organizations, school district officials, teachers, and academics in the field. However, there was a downside to surveying so many people. In an effort to accommodate the many requests made during the needs assessment, a large number of sessions were scheduled and consequently were kept short. Most offerings were a half or full day—few were longer.

Teachers' Suggestions for Content

The bulk of the suggestions by teachers relates to aspects of classroom teaching. However, then and now some favorite topics are on the personal side. Stress management and personal finance are perennials. Teaching to diversity, working with English learners, and working with students with mild to moderate disabilities were and are frequently requested. Using the computer in instruction has been mentioned often for a number of years, but there is confusion about just what that topic entails, and most computer-related sessions have tended to be for teachers' uses. Although sessions on reading and writing are often asked for and are well attended by primary teachers, the other core curriculum areas are mentioned by relatively few teachers. Generic teaching skills are included more often than curriculum and instruction in the core areas.

Organizational Needs: The Words From on High Enter the Picture

State and federal government officials and organizers for school districts found that they had many needs for communication that might lead to filling part of the smorgasbord. For example, states could decide that they wanted teachers and principals to have more knowledge about the procedures for referring students for possible special education and for developing Individual Educational Plans (IEPs). Concerns about the use of illicit drugs brought about workshops on drug use and programs, such as DARE. And districts had needs to inform staff members about enrollment, grading practices, disciplinary policies—the list is long—another reason the smorgasbords grew. No Child Left Behind contains myriad regulations and procedures, many of which have to be transformed by states and districts, and the products of that transformation needs to be communicated.

Mentoring and coaching programs are often "mandated" by legislators or officials at the federal and state levels. Curriculum standards and benchmarks appear, and dissemination beckons. National organizations promote a variety of topics.

Patterns

As we have studied the arrays of offerings in large districts, where the staff development days are run as conferences with many options, some optional and some mandated, some interesting patterns have appeared. Chiefly, that even before NCLB showed up, the majority (sometimes more than three-fourths) of the workshops offered on a day's agenda in many districts were on topics promoted or mandated by combinations of government agencies, communication needs of the district, and promotions by national organizations. Consequently, a lesser portion related to the requests by teachers.

Second, brevity was emphasized, regardless of topic. Session length became a procrustean bed in which topics were stretched or shrunk to fit the three- to six-hour periods.

Many teachers attend the "staff development conference days" expecting, despite past experience, that the content will be immediately relevant to their teaching. And many complain bitterly that about 90 percent of the workshops do *not* contain content relevant to their immediate teaching practice. *In our experience, they are right, except that the content of most of the workshops was not designed to relate to practice.*

And some of the most popular suggestions from needs surveys, ones likely to be included in the agenda, will not fill everyone's needs. For example, classroom management will appeal primarily to teachers who are having some degree of problem in managing the students. Teachers with no management problem will avoid them and also be a bit disconcerted to see them on a program of events.

Also, some schools and districts fall into the practice patterns of "turnkey" training, where someone is sent to a conference or meeting so as then to replicate what went on there with the folks back home. This often leads to didactic sessions—the turnkey has only superficial knowledge and doesn't have mastery of or skill in the content, and a talk or PowerPoint presentation results.

We also believe that the organizers have gone to some of the wells too often so that topics are repeated every year, often with the same leaders. Teaching to diversity sounds good, but in brief sessions the leaders are hard put to do more than an introduction, and those introductions can get old fast.

Serious Criticism Comes to Town

We are suggesting that eventual dissatisfaction was built into the format of the smorgasbords, and today, discontent is loudly proclaimed by the national organizations (that promoted the needs assessment some years ago) and by many of the authors who write about staff development. For example, the magazine of a large national organization proclaimed that that traditional staff development, "The sage on the stage," needed to be replaced with study groups of teachers. Another, in its magazine, said bluntly that research shows that coaches get better results than workshops.

The device of referring to the sets of sessions on staff development days as "traditional" staff development (read "bad old") is used by many contemporary authors (see, for example, Wei, Darling-Hammond, Andree, Richardson, & Orphanos, 2009), who then extol their preferred model, currently mentoring, coaching, or collaborative models such as study groups and professional learning communities. The criticism of the superficial sessions is sometimes rhetorically extended to include *any* formal staff development.

Teacher Opinion

Most teachers are positive about the professional development that relates to teaching, including the value of relatively brief sessions, although longer or linked sessions are regarded more highly. The teachers are certainly less negative than the national speakers and writers.

In NCES surveys (as in NAEP, 2004), about half report that workshops lasting from one to eight hours in all content areas (including curriculum, instruction, teaching diverse students) improved their teaching moderately or "a lot." For longer workshops, 75 percent or more indicated moderate or a lot of improvement, and another 20 percent indicated "somewhat." That is nearly everyone! Given that NCES uses a national sample of teachers whose experiences must cover a wide spectrum of offerings, the level of approval they give to staff development is remarkable.

We ourselves are affirmative about several quite different models of professional development that have distinctive and overlapping goals, but we believe that quality of execution is critical. The problems we identified earlier are real ones, and we need to address them.

Back to the Drawing Boards

We believe that the criticism of what is still one of the most widely used approaches should foster a healthy reexamination of staff development. Just because the old staff development days have deteriorated doesn't mean that staff development in general doesn't need a careful examination. Here we will concentrate on what might be done to make the professional development menus viable.

Let's proceed by working uphill. For purposes of argument, let's keep the time allotted to staff development constant and see what we can do with it in the common format of three to six days a year and then other configurations that use the same amounts of time. First, let's separate what we will call "Organizational Communication Needs" from Teaching Practices. Then, let's reorganize the study of teaching and curriculum into practices that can easily be transferred from workshop to classroom and those that require new learning during the implementation process.

Giving Organizational Communication Needs Their Own Platform

Let's begin by proposing that the sessions devoted to governmental and district communication be separated in time and organization from sessions dealing with the practice of teaching, including new curricular initiatives.

In other words, the federal and state departments of education and the central offices of school districts get their days, but they are not confused with the study of teaching and curriculum.

And, while we are at it, we might modernize organizational communication. Some states have developed interactive video facilities that can carry many kinds of messages and allow for a certain amount of "town hall" action. Many states and districts are now maintaining Web sites that contain quantities of regulations that can be accessed online. And the ICU in Iowa, among other states, is an interactive video system that can provide for dissemination, questions, and discussion.

By separating the organizational communication needs from curricular and instructional needs, one can concentrate on improving the content and process of professional development—the study of curricular and instructional practice. Let's turn to a consideration of content, where teaching practice is prominent.

The Practice of Teaching: Horizontal Transfer and Vertical Transfer of New Learning

In various fields, including education, the study of learning by practitioners has resulted in the very important distinction between horizontal and vertical transfer of something new. Essentially, practices differ in complexity and familiarity. The more complex and more unfamiliar ones require more concentration and energy if implementation is to occur.

Horizontal Transfer

Horizontal transfer refers to an easy transition from a workshop to practice in the workplace.

An example is the practice of "wait time," first developed by Mary Budd Rowe at Teachers College, Columbia University (see 1974). The essence of wait time is slowing the pace of interchange between teacher and students. After asking a question, the teacher "waits," giving the students time to formulate responses rather than appearing to rush them. The result should be more and more thoughtful and accurate responses. If wait time is explained and demonstrated in a workshop and how to study student responses is demonstrated, teachers can start using it without further ado because they are adding only a small skill to their repertoire.

Another example is learning to make productive use of classroom collections of books. McGill-Franzen and her colleagues did a nice study that illustrated the importance of staff development for what, on the surface, does not appear to be a complicated skill (McGill-Franzen, Allington, Yokoi, & Brooks, 1999). The researchers provided several hundred books to the classrooms of a number of teachers. The teachers were assigned to conditions where they received no professional development on the use of the collections with the students. Virtually no use of the collections occurred. The others were assigned to workshops they studied rationale and saw demonstrations—about 20 hours of study altogether. Without further support, the latter group of teachers made productive use of the collections, increasing student independent reading substantially. They did not have to learn complex new practices, but they could redirect ones they already possessed to the goal of increasing student reading. Note that without staff development, the collections were not properly used.

Vertical Transfer

Vertical transfer refers to the need for new learning by the practitioner *as the new learning is implemented.* In other words, the workshop can start the learning, but what is demonstrated cannot simply be imitated in the workplace. When the content of professional development is outside the normal developed repertoire of the practitioners, new skills have to be consolidated during practice. For example, teachers who do not regularly use inductive models of teaching find, as they begin to do so, that they have to develop different types of lessons and supporting materials and learn to guide the students in new ways. One has to teach oneself the ideas and skills that are between the lines of the workshop. For a description of a number of models of teaching where vertical transfer is needed, see Joyce, Weil, and Calhoun, 2009.

Knowledge and skills where transfer can take place horizontally can take less time to learn than those requiring vertical transfer, with learning often completed in one or two sessions. Those requiring vertical transfer usually need several sessions spaced apart during the period of implementation, and, as well, companionship in the school— peer coaching—has a positive effect as the teachers work through the new learnings that are necessary for a full implementation.

Two Types of Workshops

We suggest that organizers (committees of teachers and curriculum/ instruction specialists) think about the potential units of study and separate them into those where horizontal transfer will probably occur and those where vertical transfer will be needed. Then, a horizontal-transfer strand of the offerings will emerge, and workshops can be planned accordingly—long enough to cover the subject and inclusive of rationale, demonstrations, and ways of studying progress—and these can be advertised as such. *These are the workshops that promise usefulness on the proverbial Monday morning.*

But—workshops on minor teaching skills will only appear practical *if* a teacher does not already possess them and, as well, they happen to mesh well with the existing repertoire of the teacher. A well-executed session with good if simple content can miss the mark for a given teacher unless it is new to that person, is subject- and grade-appropriate, and is not too far out from that person's repertoire. And note the large role that perception can play in judging the fit of the workshops. Something may be new but not perceived as such. Something that feels exotic at first may feel more learnable a little later.

These are quite demanding criteria for just a little workshop. Getting the right match with the right stuff is tricky business, but we believe it can be engineered with surprising frequency.

A small item in planning is to consider the appropriate size of groups for various topics and processes. Many of the offerings in the professional-day menu are made to small groups—up to 20 or 30. However, sessions where something is explained and rationalized and then demonstrated through videos can be offered to much larger groups on content, *if horizontal transfer can be expected*. Moreover, good speakers with something good to say can work effectively with very large groups—they *can* be the "sage on the stage" for appropriate periods of time.

Planning Conservatively

We don't think that *anybody* believes—or *ever* believed—that a three-hour workshop, or a six-hour one, could ready anyone to practice anything more than the most simple of teaching practices. And virtually everyone knows that a complex teaching strategy requires longer study and the follow-up for which peer coaching was invented.

Simple strategies that fit repertoire do not need much follow-up from a technical point of view. However, companionship helps implementation. Pairs who attend together and share experiences enjoy their colleagueship. They do not have to observe each other to share experiences. And, should they do so, the observer is there to learn, not to supervise or correct. Both need to remember that they are novices with respect to the new skill.

One's existing repertoire affects the ease with which new learning can be transferred horizontally and the degree of support needed to manage vertical transfer. But planners should design conservatively—an extra session will not hurt anyone, but too few sessions will result in frustration. A few teachers may decide to go it alone rather than join a peer-coaching team, but that has to be their call.

Planning for Vertical Transfer

The important outcome of the long series of studies was that new curriculums and models of teaching were well within the reach of teachers and administrators—*provided* that the staff development was arranged correctly. As we discussed in Chapter 5, the learning of skills involves the study of rationale, experience with demonstrations, and planning lessons and units for implementation. But where vertical transfer is necessary, follow-up is needed, and peer-coaching teams of two and three teachers can work together and achieve transfer.

Improving Process: The Workshop Way of Learning

In any field of endeavor, whenever preservice or inservice education is being planned, the problem of making study relevant to practice has to be addressed. Professional education has long grappled with the problem. When preservice study was only one or two years long, the normal school curriculums were parallel to the K–12 curriculums, and teacher candidates developed "units" that they could implement as they began their work as teachers. Later, college and university preservice programs were exhorted to operate courses as workshops where, again, the teacher candidates would develop products that would transfer to their job settings and duties. In the 1950s , '60s, and '70s, the academic reform movement in mathematics, science, and the other curriculum areas was characterized by two-track professional development curriculums, one where, say, mathematics was studied and the other where educators generated materials for the classroom. And the workshop (the term *workshop* comes from factory language, where workshops produce artifacts and machines) movement in staff development has been strong and consistent. The critics allege that the smorgasbords are populated more by didactic sessions than operated as workshops, where theory and practice are integrated and "make and take" is the order of the day.

That situation, where it occurs, should be easy to correct. We cannot imagine conducting a workshop where application is not a major component.

Professional Learning Communities as Clients for Workshops

As professional learning communities (PLCs) become the norm in schools, many of them will find that they need to reach beyond the experience of their members and learn curricular and instructional models to add to their repertoires. Regional agencies and large districts may want to consider developing a repertoire of "workshops on demand" that PLCs can draw on. It may be that a new kind of "needs assessment" will develop as collaborative groups ask the support agencies to develop offerings that they can use in accord with their needs.

As distance offerings become richer, schedules become more flexible, and online and other mediated modules can be mixed with the variety of times available in the district setting. The current online offerings are not thrilling, although some of the packages with combinations of print and video are interesting.

Schedules for Staff Development

If part of the time investment in days of staff development were reconfigured into weekly sessions, one session a month might be devoted to organizational communication and problem solving. For example, the state of Iowa currently allots eight days of contract time per year for staff development. Eight hours per day computes to 48 hours and could be reconfigured to 90 minutes per week for the 32 weeks school is in session. Or 180 minutes biweekly. There are a good many possibilities. There could be four all-day sessions, linked together to provide substantial content implemented by collaborative effort in PLCs or peer-coaching pairs, and, additionally, a number of brief sessions, largely held in the schools, dealing with content teachers select or used for their own inquiries.

Let's look at another example from our collaborative work with school districts, this time in Saskatoon, Saskatchewan, Canada. Professional development is the core of the initiative.

An Example of Curriculum Change Made by Linking Staff Development Sessions

The study was originally reported in a paper presented to the Asian/Pacific Educational Research Association in Hong Kong: Joyce, Calhoun, Jutras, & Newlove, 2006, *The Results of a Literacy Curriculum Implemented in an Entire Education Authority of 53 Schools.*

Working with us in the study and the preparation of the report were Jim Jutras, Director of Education, and Kim Newlove, Superintendent, Saskatoon Public Schools, Saskatoon, Saskatchewan, Canada.

Here is an example where several days of training were linked together to implement a curriculum in the Saskatoon Public Schools designed to help upper elementary, middle school, and secondary students who are struggling readers. The curriculum is called Read to Succeed. Teachers nominate students between Grades 4 and 12 who are having difficulty because their reading competence is poor. The objective is to accelerate their competence, their self-esteem, and their ability to teach themselves.

Teachers volunteer to teach classes of up to 15 students that meet for 90 minutes a day, 5 days a week. The curriculum is designed around the Picture Word Inductive Model (see Chapter 5), which is oriented toward beginning readers—these students are beginning readers.

The specific procedures include . . .

- the rapid development of sight vocabulary. At first, this comes through the analysis of pictures, as described in Chapter 5.
- the inductive study of words.
- extensive reading at the developed level. And, of course, the teachers read to the students regularly.
- regular writing, largely to stimulus material and prompts.
- the study of comprehension strategies—explicit strategy instruction.

The major strands of professional development were designed to prepare a cadre of teachers who could offer training and support to the Read to Succeed teachers, to offer continuing training to those teachers, and to build an assessment team that could administer tests of performance in reading.

The cadre was brought together for several days at the beginning of the school year and again for one or two days each month. They were introduced to the curriculum with the theory-demonstration-practice paradigm and worked together as peer coaches. They were assigned to Read to Succeed sections in the schools of greatest need, and the rest of their time was occupied in support of their peers, first cotraining with the consultants and later carrying on all professional development with support from those consultants. They also worked with the consultants to analyze embedded student achievement data collected by the teachers and to bring the formal test data together and analyze it. They summarized it for the cabinet and board and for distribution to the teachers of Read to Succeed and their 53 schools. In June 2006, end-of-year data were available for a random sample of students from 56 sections (477 students altogether).

For the teachers training is provided over eight 3-hour sessions during the school year, following two days of training before school starts. The teachers maintain logs in which they record use and records of student learning of vocabulary, as well as reporting problems that need to be addressed in workshops, during which teachers are covered by other school personnel or paid substitutes. They share lessons, and they plan and use (peer coaching) and the results of assessments.

They also are prepared to administer the Gray Oral Reading Test (see Chapter 5 for a description) to assess competence in reading at the beginning and end of the school year. An assessment team made up of the cadre and other teachers and administrators administers the Gray test to a random sample of students in each section to provide an estimate of the reliability of tests given by the teachers.

Here are some summative results taken from the report to the central administration and trustees.

Entry and Response

On entry to the program, the pretest scores indicate that the average student made an annual gain of about 0.6 GLE in comprehension and 0.25 in fluency, precisely the population Read to Succeed is designed to serve. At each level, the learning history scores are similar—over their years in schools, the entering students have gained at about the rates indicated above whatever grade they are in.

Looking across the entire enrollment, the average gain in comprehension is GLE 1.3 and, in fluency, 1.15.

However, as is true in the past history of Read to Succeed, about 30 percent did not gain in this, their first year in the program. The average gain of the others was GLE 1.7 in comprehension and GLE 1.4 in fluency. In the second year the 30 percent who gained little in their first year gained at the rate of the other students in the second year. Our belief is that they required a longer time to develop habits of study and optimism—they had failed to learn for several years before Read to Succeed was initiated.

The 1.7 level of gain brings most students to a new perspective on school and school achievement. They are now learning at a decent rate and bring better literacy skills and vocabulary to their classes in the core curriculum areas.

Gender

Sixty percent of the enrollment is males. Scores at entry are similar for males and females, but females gain somewhat more, and the small difference is statistically significant. This difference persisted through the first five years of the program, and no explanation has been developed. However, the gains by the males are satisfactory.

Level of Class

Classes of third graders, fourth to sixth graders, sixth to eighth graders, and above eighth all gained about the same GLE amounts on average. The curriculum did not need to be altered to accommodate students of different ages.

Socioeconomic Status

The Read to Succeed curriculum appears to have similar effects in schools serving students from homes of various economic levels. Some of the highest-achieving sections are in schools serving the urban poor. And the sections serving students from higher socioeconomic brackets are doing very well. Similarly, students identified as having mild to moderate learning disabilities, so often linked to socioeconomic status, appear to gain equally with students not so diagnosed (see Joyce, Calhoun, Jutras, & Newlove, 2006).

We included this description to illustrate how linking workshop "days" around an initiative in a curriculum area of need can bring together teachers from the spectrum of a district's schools to approach that problem together. For the teachers, the eight half days were about the amount of workshops provided in previous years. The two days at the beginning of school were in addition to the normal pattern.

In Sum: Can the Disparaged Workshops Be Saved?

Probably the present form needs serious alteration, but there needs to be a balance between inquiry generated by PLCs in their own settings and the stimulation of externally generated ideas. And some of those workshops might be oriented toward helping the school teams conduct really good action research.

Please note that we have not made any effort to "jazz up" brief sessions that are focused on trivial content. Much of the content of the present smorgasbord can be transmitted effectively through readings and video.

Our orientation is toward joining the available sessions and focusing them on curricular and instructional innovations, like Read to Succeed, that help schools deal with serious instructional problems, such as helping struggling readers. Thus the linked-together workshop sessions become more like the curricular/instructional initiatives discussed in Chapter 5.

We believe that the way to fix the superficial workshop is not to sink it but to use the time to create more solid offerings. And, properly organized, that content can support the collaborative/cooperative mode, give support to individuals, and assist in the attempt to improve curriculums. As school staffs or groups identify areas to study that are beyond their current repertoire, we can develop "workshops" to respond to their need.

7

Embracing Both Personal and Formal Knowledge Without Being Bowled Over by Either

The Nature of Evidence

I didn't really set out to be a teacher/researcher. But it's that or let your mind go to sleep.

—our reflective observer

Districts, schools, and teachers need to focus on the outcomes they want and measure them—LOOKING FOR GAIN—in the most direct way possible. If they get large gains, that is good. Factors other than the treatment may be at work, but there are no uncontaminating controls in education. Schools exist in a cultural ocean that is more like the restless sea than a placid pond.

—our reflective observer

L et's begin by wading directly into the muddy waters where knowledge about educational practice resides and is interpreted. There is plenty of good knowledge out there and, luckily, some good ways of finding more from our practice and from formal study. We are going to argue here that the experience-derived knowledge of practitioners is important and legitimate. And we will stand up for formal evaluation and research as well. All of us are hampered because there are small amounts of programmatic research or evaluation in professional development. Those hoping that they can sift through the literature and find dozens of experimental studies will be disappointed. We need to generate many more credible evaluations and research studies.

What we call *programmatic research* is the formulation of sets of studies designed to develop the fullest knowledge possible in an area. Some studies provide descriptive information that helps clarify an issue and identifies questions worthy of inquiry. Some studies may be evaluations of techniques or interventions or the behavior of educators. Some may be highly focused tests of theory. The outcome should be considerable information and understanding beyond what was available before the formal program of inquiry was undertaken.

Nonprogrammatic research is less ambitious and may consist of a single study or evaluation. A very thorough study of schoolwide action research in 60 schools that were members of the League of Cooperating Schools and other settings found some considerable successes, *where there was substantial technical assistance* (Calhoun, 1999). Single studies in single sites could have led to the conclusion that schoolwide action research usually works or usually fails, depending on the setting that was selected for the study. Programmatic research led to Calhoun's position that no type of action research, whether conducted by individuals, small groups, or whole faculties, is guaranteed to succeed. However, with technical support, success is *probable* in each of them.

In our own work, we have conducted both programs of research and one-shot studies. We designed a single controlled study to determine the effects of increases in amounts of independent book reading on competence in reading—an evaluation of what we call the "Just Read" Program (Joyce & Weil, with Calhoun, 2008; Joyce & Wolf, 1996). The variables explored included how many books students read and whether their amounts of reading increased. Grade level and class, gender, and school were also examined. However, it was a one-time study because, in other settings where we have employed Just Read, other treatments are involved, so its effects cannot be parceled out. However, it gave us a base for judging what we could expect and information on how to improve ways of increasing independent book reading by students.

Currently we are in the midst of a programmatic series exploring the effects of the Picture Word Inductive Model with primary children and our Read to Succeed curriculum for older struggling readers. Three studies from the series are described in Chapters 5 and 6 and at the end of this one. We can assert that the model can be the core of curriculums that teach reading and writing effectively. Our current efforts are designed to try to make those curriculums stronger.

Types of Evidence

There is a good deal of useful knowledge that we can consider as we seek to develop effective staff development, and not all of it is from formal studies. We will consider

1. individual personal/professional knowledge,

2. pooled professional knowledge in small groups and faculties,

3. information and concepts developed through descriptive inquiry, and

4. information from controlled studies where approaches to curriculum, teaching, staff development, and school improvement are tested and their underlying theories and assumptions can be assessed.

All four of these types of knowledge have implications for the development of professional development initiatives.

1. Personal Experience and Knowledge

As all of us work, we gain experience, and we think about that experience. Those thoughts become a major part of our professional knowledge. Some of these ideas are right on the surface, and we can express them easily. Some reside comfortably below the surface, and we don't talk about them much.

The products of personal experience are very important. We carry them with us as we live and work. We develop principles that guide our planning and action in teaching and administration. Personal knowledge should not be deprecated or spoken of as minor because it comes from the mind of only one person and has not been tested formally. And, when push comes to shove, we have to trust our minds, even while being aware of our fallibility. Borrowing Dave Hunt's words, "Teachers are their own best theorists."

We engage in various kinds of professional activities—teaching and organizing—because we believe they will work. As individuals, we do not—certainly should not—believe that we have the *only* ideas that might work, but they are *our* ideas and help us face each day's work and the tasks within those days with the product of our brains to guide us. Primary teachers teach reading with those ideas. Physics teachers do the same. Any learning that we do as a product of professional development needs to be reconciled with our personal educational psychology and educational philosophy. We defend these ideas and can do so fiercely if they are treated carelessly. But we need not build our defenses so high that we fail to keep our ideas growing. Studying them is tricky but essential.

2. Pooled Professional Knowledge and Experience

Pooled personal experiences and knowledge are also *very* important. Despite the traditional isolation of teachers and administrators, we do interact with one another; we exchange ideas, and the ideas of others rub off on us. At the very least, those ideas help us process information a little differently and help us understand problems a bit better. Most important, we pick up ideas and ways of thinking so that we grow from our interchanges. The models of professional development that work by generating professional learning communities depend heavily on the benefits of pooled knowledge and skill. In learning communities we react to the ideas and practices of others, borrowing some and rejecting others. Our personalities and states of growth affect the ease with which we consider the ideas and activities of others and learn from them. Again, the action research paradigm can help group inquiry, but just the interaction helps us test our ideas and try to build on them.

3. Information From Descriptive Studies

As we squeeze our experience for personal knowledge and borrow ideas and skills from our colleagues, we can also obtain information and concepts from formal lines of inquiry. They then become part of our storehouse.

Formal inquiry, particularly long-term programmatic study, endeavors to probe aspects of the educational process and clarify factors that operate. Optimally we reflect on our personal knowledge and bounce it off the frames of reference that are developed as formal inquiry takes place and tests the products of our experience. Descriptive studies can both clarify and illuminate.

Tennis, Anyone? An Illustration

Let's illustrate what can happen with an excursion into the game of tennis and how personal knowledge can interact with formal study. Imagine two couples who play tennis regularly on Saturday afternoons, weather permitting. Let's call one couple Fred and Ginger and the other Nick and Nora. In terms of general capability—quality of strokes, reliability of serves, and fitness—the two couples are about even. If you observe them as they warm up before playing, you would find that they look about equally skillful and comfortable on the tennis court. The individuals get along well as couples, and the couples get along with each other very well.

As they play, we find that the pooled knowledge of the two partnerships differs in a way that affects how they play doubles. Fred and Ginger have decided that they are most effective when, as play develops, one covers the front of the court (the part closest to the net) and the other covers the back part of the court.

Nick and Nora play parallel to one another. When one is in the front of the court, the other is more or less by his or her side. They move forward and back together.

Something happens that mystifies them, especially Fred and Ginger, because Ginger and Fred lose most of the matches the couples play. And, after a match, they feel that Nick and Nora made more of the best strokes, and that is, objectively, true. They all make some good shots, but Fred and Ginger make fewer.

Formal Knowledge

When we look at descriptive studies by formal researchers of tennis, we find some concepts that help explain what has been going on with Fred and Ginger and Nick and Nora. That is, the geometry of a tennis court and the physics of positioning strongly favor doubles teams who play parallel to one another. In fact, the parallel players will win as many as three out of four points from approximately equal opponents (Braden & Burns, 1977).

If our couples attend a series of lessons on doubles strategy (the equivalent of staff development in tennis), these concepts will come out, and the instructor will give special attention to teaching Fred and Ginger to play parallel to one another. As they learn to do so, they will gradually win more of the matches and find that they are in position to hit better shots, other factors remaining relatively equal. The teams will almost magically become about equal because of the use of formal knowledge.

Here is a clear case where descriptive research, in this case focused on describing the behavior of teams in doubles matches, can have an effect. Winning teams whose basic strokes and fitness were similar to the losing teams employed the parallel pattern. The product is teachable.

A Parallel (No Pun Intended) in Educational Practice

The yield from descriptive studies can help us augment our personal and pooled knowledge. Most often descriptive work adds to our points of view rather than correcting us. Sometimes formal studies help us see things from a different angle that helps us better understand our personal experience. Sometimes we encounter ideas that challenge our present ones.

We can't describe the entire yield of descriptive research in all the areas that have been studied. Let's look at one where descriptive work has provided information that can be useful to all of us as we try to improve schooling and the professional development on which progress depends.

Beliefs About Capacity: The World of Expectations

One of the most perplexing questions in educational practice has to do with the extent to which the characteristics of the students affect their learning. A mass of correlational evidence from descriptive research supports the propositions that

- the socioeconomic status of students is strongly associated with learning in most schools and districts,

- aptitude scores (read IQ) are correlated with achievement, and
- the presence of learning disabilities is negatively correlated with later achievement.

Given the regularity of these findings, we can easily understand the origins of the common belief that the characteristics of our students outweigh our styles of teaching in determining how much is learned. Whom we get to teach, rather than how we teach, appears to be responsible for student learning. This belief is reinforced by findings from the evaluations of some large-scale programs designed to interrupt the influence of those factors. In the United States, most Title I and special education programs have had either small effects or, frequently, none.

However, a number of lines of formal inquiry have provided concepts that put those correlations into a different light by looking closely at the relationships between perceptions of students and the diets of curriculum and instruction that are provided to them.

First, it appears that that how we regard the students, particularly how we regard their capacity, affects the educational diets we provide them. The more capable we believe they are, the more complex and stimulating the curriculums and ways of teaching we provide to them. And the better they respond, the more they learn. In other words, the more highly regarded the students, the more stimulating the educational environments that we provide, and the better the effects.

The tricky item here is that it is our *beliefs* about the students that affect *our* behavior. If we *believe* the students are capable, we treat them as such, and the effects are that the students come to believe in themselves as capable. As they do, they behave more competently, and the consequences are good.

Programs for the economically poor students and for "special education" students both labor under the negative effects of the expectations-effects circular effect. Essentially, successful programs are carried by the belief that, contrary to surface appearances, the poor and disabled students are capable. Success occurs *because* the students can learn and because, believing that, educators provide content-rich and nurturing environments.

A Caution

Sometimes descriptive research is undervalued in education because it does not prove causation. And, because of its roots in scientific inquiry, medicine is often cited as an area based on classic experimental designs rather than on descriptive research. Not so. Descriptive research is abundant in the medical base, and we have an example close at hand. At the moment we are editing this section, we are sitting in a waiting room in the Mayo Clinic in Jacksonville, Florida. On the table next to us lies a report on obesity from the Mayo Clinic Newsletter that describes studies that link obesity to a number of debilitating conditions. The recommendations for our health are stated strongly. This is medical advice based on descriptive research. But the researchers did not make a controlled sample of fat people to prove causation before recommending that we have more than cosmetic reasons to control our weight. Similarly, our concerns about smoking do not come from experimental studies where we taught a certain number of subjects to smoke so we could collect data on the consequences. However, we can infer from the correlations that smoking and obesity should be avoided if possible.

That said, the study of interventions, in the helping professions—medicine, education, therapy—involves implementing treatments and studying the effects. The effort includes not only trying to make the results clear but also learning whether variables other than the treatments might have caused the results.

4. Educational Practice-Oriented Research: Design, Inferences, Warrants

Evaluation and research are not identical. Let's look first at evaluation.

Design of Evaluations

When a teacher, faculty, or district makes a change in practice with goals in mind, it needs to try to find out whether those goals were achieved. The common change in secondary schools called "block scheduling" is an example. Essentially, periods of instruction are lengthened. Evaluating block scheduling focuses on two questions: Did the teaching/learning process change? Did student learning change (were course objectives better achieved)? The control can be teaching/learning behavior and student achievement in the years immediately past. A treatment versus no treatment experimental design is not necessary. However, any positive effects may be due to factors other than changing the length of instructional periods. For example, students are enrolled in fewer courses, which might help them concentrate on the content. (A follow-up study might ask the students if that was the case.) However, if there are few changes in instruction or achievement, it would be hard to claim that the change made a positive difference.

Although a simple design does not rule out factors other than the treatment, it is worthwhile and important. Many districts have instituted block scheduling because it is highly publicized but have not conducted their own evaluations. Those who have conducted them have much more information about whether to continue the practice.

Evaluations of initiatives in schools and school districts need to focus on the nature and effects of curriculums, ways of teaching, and the social climate provided to the students. But districts need not try to rule out all competing variables, and often it would be impractical to try. And schools are places of teaching and learning. Laboratory-style research can be set up temporarily to test a theory or practice, but making a school laboratory-pure would be like taking the air out of it. However, evaluations should be done carefully and with a eye on variables that might confound findings.

The evaluations of professional development models need to concentrate on resulting teacher behavior before proceeding to incorporate measures of student learning. Frequently staff development "evaluations" consist of the use of opinionaires after workshops or meetings of professional learning communities. There is little correlation between attitudes toward sessions and the use of new practice. Actual change has to be studied.

Design of Research in Field Settings

In Chapter 5 we identified sets of programmatic investigations into curriculum and instruction and school renewal and training. Substantial quantities of such research exist, and the results can guide decision making about initiatives both in schooling and in staff development.

Here we will concern ourselves with the creation of designs that enable a professional development practice to be tested as schooling takes place.

The core of research into whether particular practices make a difference is to test those practices by using them under conditions that enable the assessment of effects to take place and reduce the possibility that any results are due to another cause.

Designing studies of educational treatments in field settings involves careful efforts to build in controls, including

- clarifying the treatment and its rationale;
- designing and implementing adequate professional development;

- studying implementation—verifying that the teachers have learned the treatment, can use it, and do use it;
- studying effects formatively if possible; and
- studying effects against a baseline. Frequently this involves measuring performance before, during, and at the end of the period of study. When tests are used, those administering them will have to be prepared to do so reliably.

Using these controls is straightforward but takes energy and, despite best efforts, almost always is flawed.

A Prototype Effort

Suppose we want to test a curricular or instructional strategy, a variation in social climate, or a staff development procedure, and the purpose of the procedure is to cause specific effects on student learning. We should begin with a study with a relatively small sample. (Actually, our Saskatoon studies were much larger than the size we recommend for first studies.)

We begin with a cooperative, perhaps collaborative, school district. Within a given elementary school grade, say fifth grade, we identify 20 classrooms randomly. We assign, again randomly, ten classrooms to our treatment and ten as controls.

We provide extensive training to the teachers of *both* groups. The content for the treatment group is the curricular/instructional strategy designed to generate the particular effects that are the focus of our study. The control group teachers receive training on a generic curricular strategy where the treatment effects are not targeted but the control strategy has relevance to the curriculum area of which the treatment is a part. For example, if the treatment content is skills for comprehending text, the control might be wider reading from classroom collections, as in the McGill-Franzen, Allington, Yokoi, and Brooks study described in Chapter 6.

A pretest, focused on the treatment outcome, is given to the students in both groups.

Let's suppose the treatment period is six months—October to March. Past research on curriculum and instruction has indicated that a period of that length is sufficient for treatment effects to show up. If they haven't appeared in that amount of time, they rarely will do so. In our case, the test will be given in October.

During implementation the teachers report their levels of use of the content of the training, and observers visit and estimate levels of use.

The posttest is given in March.

Calculations of effect: Gain scores are calculated for each student, the treatment group and control group are compared, and level of use is taken into account.

Why does the control group get a treatment? Because the fact of training might affect the behavior of the teachers. For example, it might engender energy that could be responsible for effects on the students.

It is possible to use a second control group that gets no training but where the pretests and posttests are given to the students. Doing so helps provide some more information about whether the presence of training itself makes a difference, but it is not a perfect solution: Just giving the pretest can orient teachers to the purpose of the study and induce them to put forth extra energy and time in the targeted area.

Why do we prefer small studies for initial tests of a procedure? Because we can generate substantial training and study implementation thoroughly.

We favor precision over size. In the hypothetical case above, were we to replicate it and get about the same findings, we would come closer to confidence in our treatment.

Very Large-Scale Studies: Issues in Implementation

Let's look at two examples of large-scale studies. In the first, teaching reading comprehension is the focus, and professional development is the vehicle that generates the treatments. In the second, the effectiveness of a professional development model in the form of new teacher induction, centered on mentoring, is tested. Here, professional development is important in two places, as it is provided to the mentors and the mentors provide service to new teachers.

Reading Comprehension

In this study 89 schools were selected in 10 districts from several states, and the content was comprehension strategies in reading. The teachers involved were 268 in number, and 6,350 students were tested. The control teachers were asked to use their customary teaching strategies during the period of the study. The treatment was skill in comprehending text (James-Bardurny, Mansfield, Deke, Carey, Lugo-Gil, Hershey, Douglas, Gersten, Newman-Gonchar, Dimino, Faddis, & Pendleton, 2009).

Imagine the complexity of the logistics to implement training thoroughly! Even testing so many students in so many settings can involve uncontrolled variance!

The training model they used is not clearly described, but the amounts are 12 hours of initial training and 7½ hours of follow-up training.

The investigators reported data on implementation. First, over 90 percent of the control teachers actually participated in training. Of these, 56 to 80 percent reported that they were well prepared to use the content of the training. Observers reported that 55–78 percent of the new behaviors were seen during their visits.

Nonetheless, in reports disseminated by the U.S. Office of Education, the conclusion is that the treatment content "made no difference" to relevant student learning. Are they convincing?

We conduct professional development on reading and writing comprehension strategies and are highly skeptical that the small amount of training was sufficient to carry the content; also the implementation rates are below those we would find acceptable.

In its "quick review" of the study, the comment is included that "the analysis of teacher outcomes described in this report is consistent with WWC [What Works Clearinghouse] evidence standards." The What Works administrators place a high premium on random assignment and on a scale of study that includes several districts and reaches across states. Quality of training, level of implementation, and precision of membership are not as heavily emphasized.

Professional Development: Teacher Induction and, Therefore, Mentoring

The same company (Mathematica) recently reported another very large-scale study from which it concludes that mentoring made no difference in whether new teachers stayed in their schools or stayed in teaching (Glazerman, Dolfin, Bleeker, Johnson, Isenberg, Lugo-Gel, Grider, & Britton, 2009).

The size of the study is amazing. It included more than 1,000 teachers in 418 elementary schools, mostly serving low-SES neighborhoods, in 17 school districts in several states.

The new teachers in half the schools were assigned mentors prepared to use the comprehensive teacher induction (CTI) program, which includes a weekly meeting with the mentor and observations with constructive feedback.

The detailed report is not yet available, but the U.S. Office of Education has publicized two findings. One is that 75 percent of the teachers in both treatment and control conditions returned to their schools for another year. The induction programs did not have lower figures of retention in school. The other finding is that 95 percent of both groups remained in teaching, some in other schools in their first district and some in schools in other districts. The induction program did not have lower figures of retention in teaching.

It may be that the loss of 5 percent may be close to an *irreducible minimum.* If 95 percent of the control group of teachers, most of whom were working in Title I schools, continued in teaching, we could hardly expect supplementary mentoring to increase that amount very much.

Again, we suspect that amounts and quality of preparation of mentors and degrees of implementation were factors, although the investigators spent considerable energy organizing training and studying implementation. The teachers who were in the supplementary induction programs did report receiving more attention in visits by mentors and professional development workshops.

Issues of Quality

We worry about quality control in the large-scale studies. Sometimes poor quality implementation occurs, often leading to the "no significant difference" conclusion because training, implementation, and testing are too weak to show effects from *any* intervention. Essentially, without an enormous effort to ensure high quality in a large-scale study, the treatment may be watered down to almost nothing, or the control may get relevant support.

In this study, the teachers in the control situations were not without *any* support. In education you simply cannot have a control where the students are in suspended animation—something will be happening to them, and that something can support growth. Only where the goal is knowledge or skill that is exotic with respect to normal experience can we be fairly sure that the control students will not learn it while we are not looking. In our recent studies in kindergarten reading, we *know* that in those schools, only one or two students in a class will usually learn to read unless they are taught in school. So learning to read is a school function. But it is always possible that we will run into a situation where all the parents decide to teach their little ones to read.

To illustrate our own struggle to deal with quality in a study of size, we will look at one of our collaborations with the Saskatoon, Canada, public schools—a large-scale professional development-driven initiative in literacy. We use this work as an illustration because we have intimate knowledge of it and can provide information about why certain types of control were used. We can also acknowledge the imperfections that we are aware of rather than reporting the work of someone else and critiquing it.

Some of the descriptions provided in the studies reported in Chapters 5 and 6 are relevant here; they will not be repeated but will be referred to where appropriate.

Literacy for All in Saskatoon: An Initiative and a Study

A note on the school district:

It is located in Saskatoon, a city of 210,000 people. Saskatoon is the largest city in the province of Saskatchewan, Canada. The Saskatoon Public School District has 43 (K–8) elementary schools and nine collegiates (9–12), plus a K–12 associated school. There are more than 1,200 professional staff and 450 teaching assistants who serve nearly 21,000 students. Ten elementary schools and three secondary schools are designated as "community" schools, which receive special fiscal and human resources because their students, due to socioeconomic circumstances, may be at particular risk. First Nations, Metis, and Inuit students compose 18 percent of the student body. Ten trustees, each representing a ward (voting section) of the city, make up the governing board. Many teachers and administrators collaborated with us. Jim Jutras, Kim Newlove, and Lori and Ralph Kindrachuk were key collaborators, and all the members of the "Literacy Teachers" cadre were particularly important to the initiative and study.

What happens if the trustees of a district and the administrative officers believe that divisionwide initiatives need to be made to impel student learning beyond the vision of each school-based community of teachers? What happens if they make initiatives based on scholarship about how to build better curriculums? In other words, what if prototype curriculums are scaled up to reach students across the division?

Although in the public school division of Saskatoon we do support school-based learning communities, the central story here is of an extensive set of initiatives that we refer to collectively as the Literacy for Life program.

Deciding on Literacy for Life

The decision did not emanate from a general belief or evidence that literacy was in bad shape in the division or a public outcry for improvement. Although there has long been a recognized need to increase student achievement in the schools serving lower SES populations and ethnic minorities, that condition was not unusual in Canada or the United States. We were not in the kind of situation where everyone was shouting that we needed to "close the gap." In fact, the district had made substantial initiatives to provide greater resources to the lower-achieving schools, improve community and parental involvement, and provide richer experiences for the students. These provisions were based on conventional wisdom, but they were substantial. *Complacency* is too strong a word to describe how both public and professionals felt about the condition of education, but it is not too far off.

However, a dawning awareness that things could be better began to spread through the professional staff.

A precipitating event occurred when a group of elementary principals and central office staff visited the Northern Lights school division, observed teachers, talked with teachers and administrators, and studied the results of their initiative. They were impressed with the energy and enthusiasm they found and their apparent effects on the diverse population of students. They took their findings to the Saskatoon Public School District central administration and trustees. It turned out that, under the contented surface of feelings about the state of education, many people, including the trustees, worried about the unevenness of achievement in the division.

Following considerable discussion, the trustees and professional leaders decided to make a strong push in the literacy area for several years. A core planning group of central office personnel met with a team of consultants to generate a plan based on research on staff development and innovations in literacy learning. The program we describe below emerged from the discussions and was named "Literacy for All."

The component initiatives of literacy for life:

A strong effort to build a divisionwide learning community is combined with curriculum development and an action research frame of reference toward school improvement, staff development, and the study of student learning.

Here we see the fleshing out of the initiative and the process of designing and implementing substantial professional development.

Here we see the effort to . . .

- *Clarify the treatment and its rationale.* The core ideas had to be understood by the organizers—policymakers, central office leaders, and lead principals—and effectively disseminated to hundreds of professional teachers and thousands of parents and community members. Each year about 240 kindergarten and first- and second-grade classes and 50–60 sections of Read to Succeed were involved, serving about 1,500 kindergarten students, 1,400

first-grade, and 1,400 second-grade students (the entire populations), and about 800 Grade 4–12 struggling readers.

- *Build a sense of unity and common purpose across the division's profes-sional staff.* This was a major objective, balancing the "site-based" and school-based "learning community" frame of reference that had been established in the district for many years. As described below, all schools participated in an initiative (Just Read) to increase independent reading by all students. All schools initiated sections of a safety net program for older (Grades 3 to 12) struggling readers and writers (Read to Succeed). All kindergarten, first-grade, and second-grade teachers were studying a new repertoire for teaching reading and writing and collecting data about the effects on student learning.
- *Establish a districtwide action-research style of professional work.* In the component strands of Literacy for Life, data collection and analysis are built in. Also, a cadre of assessors (teachers and administrators) had been developed to conduct formal assessments of student learning beyond what the classroom teachers routinely collected as they study student progress in alphabet recognition, vocabulary development, and writing.
- *Conduct extensive research-based and action-research-oriented staff development.* Just Read and Read to Succeed are based on studies of how literacy is developed and on previous evaluations of prototype compo-nents. The models of teaching and curriculum that were the content of the kindergarten, first-grade, and second-grade initiatives are grounded in theory and research that has been conducted on those models.
- *Develop a cadre of teachers who can provide staff development and tech-nical support to their colleagues.* This component was designed to build a professional development cadre in the school division and to avoid a dependency connection on the external consultants who, of necessity, provided the initial training.

The primary strands that change the learning environment of the students included . . .

a. Kindergarten curriculum and instruction, where all teachers were study-ing a new set of teaching models, particularly the Picture Word Inductive Model (PWIM) (Calhoun, 1999), for teaching reading and writing (described in Chapter 5). Teachers collected data on students' alphabet recognition, acquisition of sight vocabulary, and other aspects of learn-ing to read and write. Simultaneously, teachers completed implementa-tion logs about the curriculum and their use of the models. The information from these logs and the student data was analyzed and used in planning staff development sessions, studying the quality of imple-mentation, and studying the effects districtwide on students.

> Here we see the effort to bring about the study of implementation—verifying that the teachers have learned the treatment, can use it, and do use it and conducting the formative study of effects.

  b. First-grade curriculum and instruction, where again the core is the PWIM model, including extensive reading and writing and explicit strategy instruction in comprehension and composing think-alouds (metacognitive training) in writing.

  c. Second-grade curriculum and instruction, with the above strategies, plus the use of concept attainment and inductive models of teaching to strengthen students' sentence and paragraph structures (see Joyce & Weil, with Calhoun, 2008).

  d. Read to Succeed, where more than 60 sections serve about 800 struggling readers from Grades 3 to 12, with "overage beginning readers" being taught using the same curriculums and models of teaching described above—curriculum and models that are generally confined to on-age beginning readers (see Joyce, Calhoun, & Hrycauk, 2001; see also the discussion in Chapter 6).

  e. Just Read, whose purpose is to increase at-home independent reading at the developmental level for all students and to instigate action research on reading by students, parents, teachers, schools, and the division (see Joyce & Wolf, 1996; Wolf, 1998).

Extensive staff development accompanied each of the initiatives.

Also, evaluation of student learning was embedded in each of them. Included were the regular collection of data by the teachers and periodic formal assessments by a team of specially trained assessors. During the first year, all first-grade teachers and the teachers of 65 Read to Succeed sections received ten days of staff development in workshops. During the second year, all first- and second-grade and Read to Succeed teachers received eight to nine days of training, and kindergarten teachers participated in about ten days of training.

The Design of Training and the Study of Implementation

The staff development model developed and researched by Joyce and Showers (2002) and described in Chapter 5 was employed with adaptations to the realities of the school district structure and setting. An extensive library of videotapes was available to use in the presentation of demonstrations and in explorations of rationale. The training sessions were structured so that the teachers from the 43 elementary schools could share what were they doing.

The teachers studied their implementation of the selected models, using logs that dealt with various aspects of the curriculum, including certain types of student learning (categories developed, sight vocabulary learned, types of sentences generated, etc.). The staff development team studied these logs to provide a base for modulating training and for estimating levels of implementation. Those estimates could be used to determine the overall success of the effort, as measured by implementation levels, and to correlate levels of implementation with measures of student learning where that type of analysis was appropriate.

Summative Measures of Student Learning

In this "scaling up" experiment, involving the entire division faculty for Just Read and intensive work by 80 kindergarten, 80 first-grade, 80 second-grade, and 70 Read to Succeed teachers, student achievement was a critical objective, even though the organizational and social purposes were important as well. The K–2 and Read to Succeed initiatives reached over 4,000 students, and Just Read reached all 20,000 students. Unlike school improvement approaches where the organizational climate is improved with the expectation that school improvement initiatives will follow (see Schmoker, 2006), this effort utilized substantive initiatives to build a more synergistic school improvement climate (see Joyce, Calhoun, & Hopkins, 1999). Assessment became an important part of building a districtwide action research community (see Calhoun, 1994).

The Assessment Cadre

A cadre of central office personnel, principals, and teachers (the literacy cadre mentioned above) received training in the administration of the Gunning Procedure (Gunning, 1998) and the Gray Oral Reading Test (GORT) (Wiederholt & Bryant, 2001). All school principals studied the administration of the GORT. The kindergarten and first-grade teachers studied student learning of the alphabet, sight vocabulary, and student writing. Schools studied, weekly, the amounts of independent reading done by their students.

Student Learning Results From Formal Assessments

The data reported here are from the formal assessments in late spring 2006, with some comparisons from the ends of previous years. Controls are from previous years or norms of tests. Sampling was used, with several students drawn from each class or section of each initiative. Kindergarten, first-grade, and second-grade results are presented here. Read to Succeed was discussed and results presented in Chapter 6.

Kindergarten. In the past only a handful of the division students had learned to read in the kindergarten year, and by the beginning of first grade, only about a quarter of the students had 100 percent alphabet recognition.

At the end of this kindergarten year, only 1 student (of 350 tested) had not reached the Picture Level or above.

Picture Level—30 percent

Caption Level—34 percent

Easy Sight—12 percent

One of the Beginning Reading Levels—18 percent

Level 2-A—6 percent

This was a very promising picture. And it augured well for the future. Thirty-six percent of the students were at the Easy Sight Level or better. In the past, many students had left first grade without that much competence. The Level 2-A readers are on a par with many middle elementary grade students.

Grade One. In May and June, the Gray Oral Reading Test was administered to the first-grade students by the assessment cadre.

Two years previously a similar assessment had resulted in a mean of 1.6 Grade Level Equivalent (GLE). One year previously the same procedure had resulted in a mean of about GLE 2.2. The mean for this year was about 2.4. Only about 15 percent of the students were below GLE 1.8 (which could be called achieving "grade level"), whereas 70 percent had been below that level in the assessment of first-grade students two years earlier.

Grade Two. The tests for the second-grade students were given after just seven of the ten months of the school year had elapsed, and in test terms, there were three months left. In the GORT norms on the comprehension dimension of reading, the average score for North American students is about 2.7 GLE after seven months. That average includes all students, including students from the highest- and lowest-achieving schools in Canada and the United States. The sample of 215 second-grade students was sufficient to estimate effects for second-grade students at an 0.01 level.

Here, the average was 3.0. The difference between this result and the average of 2.7 GLE was the equivalent of about a third of a year of schooling. Conservatively, with three months of school remaining, their average would be about 3.4, or about four months above the scores for second-grade students in general.

Gender. Usually females learn to read earlier and better than males. The difference widens until about 60 percent of students enrolled in higher education are females. What is our picture here?

Essentially, there was no significant difference between these second-grade boys and girls. This fits with historical results when these curriculum and instructional components were combined/implemented. As achievement rises, so does equity.

Reflections

The job is not done. Some students still will leave second grade with serious gaps in their competency to read. However, the second-grade results are positive, and we are working to accelerate the literacy development of those students who are needy. Read to Succeed will net some of them. But for the future, we hope that three years of intensive reading instruction in K–2 will result in fewer numbers of struggling students each year.

As we leave our discussions of knowledge and evidence, we can ask . . .

- Were the effects solely due to the curricular and instructional changes?
- Could the affirmative organizational climate have been a factor, as it was in the Iowa school board studies we discussed in Chapters 2 and 5?
- Would this effort replicate in another setting?
- Clearly elements of several models of professional development were combined here. Could the effort have been successfully designed with just one model? Or two?

8

The Importance of Cockeyed Optimism

Proceeding With Pride and Confidence

Questions from our reflective observer:

> *Why do we usually give end-of-year tests but rarely use beginning-of-year pretests so we can calculate gain?*
>
> *Are we stubborn? Surely not all of us are that stubborn.*
>
> *My principal is a great mentor and coach and a specialist in literacy. Does she have to hire another mentor or literacy coach?*
>
> *Why are three-fifths of our college and university students females, and why are their average grades higher than the male average?*

A t this point no one should be surprised that institutional change comes down to changing ourselves. Unless someone believes that professional development is perfect, we have to fan the winds of change—in our own direction.

The good news is that the combination of experiential knowledge and formal study provide, between them, a decent base to work from.

The most daunting thing about educational improvement is that the doggoned enterprise is so huge. And its problems, like providing equity despite SES differences, is that the SES machinery is society-wide and culturally embedded. But we cannot be intimidated by the sheer size and complexity of the enterprise. Each of us has to concentrate on making our environment a good one for our development and that of our colleagues. If we each keep our own house humming, the village will look very good.

Curricular and instructional knowledge is sufficient that we have the tools to teach all subjects in such a way that 21st-century skills—components of intelligence—are developed.

We have tried to provide some ideas that can help the commonly used models work well, and we revisit some of them here:

> Central is the idea that there are numerous legitimate approaches to generating growth opportunities for educators.

> Second is the assertion that these approaches, while often having overlapping goals, such as helping all of us attain higher states of growth, favor certain goals of their own. We are not going to have "one best model" but a variety that can, in combination, have a fine impact.

> Third is the idea, backed up by much research, that teachers have the learning capacity to profit from any of these models, provided that they are implemented well. That does not mean that choosing a model is not important—different ones will take you in different directions.

> Fourth, teachers are not identical, and their states of growth and conceptual development have much to do with what and how much they learn from a given experience and environment.

> Fifth, developing charters to elevate the organizational climates of schools should help all approaches to fulfill their mission well. The climate of the school is a critical factor.

> Sixth, the assessment of student learning should be continuous and formative and based on measures of performance. We have illustrated this in the studies we summarized at the end of Chapters 5, 6, and 7 rather than providing a didactic section on this topic. We will say here that schools do not need control groups to evaluate the progress of their students. Good evaluation tells us about gains, not whether those gains could have been

achieved in another way or in another setting. If all your students can write strongly and attractively, you have achieved a goal. Someone else might, also, but that is not the point of evaluation, which is to learn whether we achieve our goals. Students might develop certain skills without *any* teaching, but we do not have the option of closing school for a year or two to have "no teaching" as a control. Using regional or national norms, as we did with the Gray Oral Reading Test in our illustrations, can help us understand our progress, and those norms provide a surrogate control. And measuring gain—looking at where the students began and where they progress to—is very important. Essentially, where the students begin is the control.

Seventh, the principals we will hire will have the knowledge and skills to lead curricular and instructional improvement, which depends on their leadership of a fine professional development program. The principal will have the knowledge and skill to be a really good mentor and coach and the know-how to train mentors and coaches. Whatever other areas of curricular competence he or she may have, the principal will be an expert on the teaching of reading and writing and able to conduct formal professional development in literacy. He or she will be able to lead other administrators, faculty, *and* parents in the development of charters.

Does this list give you a clear idea of the professional development strands for the principalship?

Not to mention a picture of the competencies needed by any of us who would be leaders in this field.

A Final Note

Our goal is to develop transportable models of professional development— ways of making its varieties strong and successful, creating new and effective initiatives within the garden of current varieties—and moving toward a full-service human resource development system in education. Our inquiry starts with a considerable trek through the contemporary literature and practice to grasp what is being done— identifying the present models that guide best practice and on which, perhaps, we can create new ones.

Studies comparing various models of staff development on the same outcomes are impractical, because those models have different goals aside from the general objective of ultimately improving the climate of the school and the learning of students.

A Better Question to Ask of Evaluation and Research: What Might Be Good for What?

Each staff development model can be good for some goals but is probably not good for all goals.

We are concerned by a characteristic of some of the literature on staff development, which is a style where current practice is bashed, then the "new" practice is trumpeted as the savior. Best, we think, is to assume goodwill and intelligence on the part of everyone who aspires to help educators live a better professional life. We need to make things better—yes we do.

Mistakes Easy to Make

A common mistake is to assume that most personnel already know all the options for curriculum and teaching and how to implement them.

Another is to assume that involving staff members in decision making automatically generates positive motivation. Nearly all school systems involve teachers and principals in the planning of the staff development that is so heavily criticized today.

Just because teachers are good learners, it does not follow that staff development can be short and lightly delivered. Learning new curricular and instructional procedures takes hard work.

During the administration of the No Child Left Behind frame of reference, the government insistence on "high-stakes" testing with traditional multiple-choice formatted "standardized" tests to evaluate student learning has had some worrisome side effects. Among them is to draw schools into teaching those things that can be measured by multiple-choice tests and, consequently, moving education away from conceptual approaches to the core curriculum areas. Schools and districts, even states, can add performance-based tests to provide a balance of information and help legitimize the teaching of the more important dimensions of the core curriculum areas.

As to research, we are drawn to the perspective of Abraham Kaplan (Kaplan, 1964/1998), whose studies of the methodology of the behavioral sciences cover all the related disciplines and subdisciplines. As he introduces his inquiry, he comments,

> This book will contain no definition of "scientific method," whether for the study of man or for any other science.... because I believe there is no one thing to be defined.... One could as well speak of "the method" for baseball. There are ways of pitching, hitting, and running bases; ways of fielding;

managerial strategies for pinch hitters and relief pitchers; ways of signaling, coaching, and maintaining team spirit. All of these, and more besides, enter into playing the game well, and each of them has an indefinite number of variants. We could say, of course, that there is only one way to play: to score runs if you are batting, and to prevent them if you are not. And this statement would be about as helpful as any general and abstract definition of "scientific method." ... If we are to do justice to complexity, I think it is hard to improve on P. W. Bridgman's remark that "the scientist has no other method than doing his damnedest." (Kaplan, p. 27).

References

Bean, R., & Deford, D. (2008). *Dos and don'ts for literacy coaches: Advice from the field*. Portland, OR: Northwest Regional Educational Laboratory.

Borg, W., Langer, P., & Gall, M. (1970). *The minicourse: A microteaching approach to education*. Beverly Hills, CA: Collier-Macmillan.

Bredderman, T. (1983). Effects of activity-based elementary science on student outcomes: A quantitative synthesis. *Review of Educational Research, 53*(4), 499–518.

Brooks, D. (2005, October 16). Mind over muscle. *The New York Times*, p. A-12.

Calhoun, E. (1994). *How to use action research in the self-renewing school*. Alexandria, VA: Association for Supervision and Curriculum Development.

Calhoun, E. (1999). *Teaching beginning reading and writing with the Picture Word Inductive Model*. Alexandria, VA: Association for Supervision and Curriculum Development.

Calhoun, E., & Glickman, C. (1993, April). *Issues and dilemmas of action research in the League of Professional Schools*. Paper presented at the annual meeting of the American Educational Research Association, Atlanta, GA. (ERIC Document Reproduction Service No. ED360327)

Corey, S. (1953). *Action research to improve school practice*. New York: Teachers College Press.

Darling-Hammond, L., Wei, R., Andree, A., Richardson, N., & Orphanos, S. (2009). *Professional learning in the learning profession: A status report on teacher development in the United States and abroad*. Dallas, TX: National Staff Development Council. (Despite the similarity of titles, this is not the technical report on which this article is based.)

Deshler, D., & Schumaker, J. (2006). *Teaching adolescents with disabilities*. Thousand Oaks, CA: Corwin.

Donahue, P. (1999). *1998 NAEP reading report card for the nation and the states*. Washington, DC: U.S. Department of Education.

Durkin, D. (1966). *Children who read early: Two longitudinal studies*. New York: Teachers College Press.

Elkind, D. (1987). *Miseducation: Preschoolers at risk*. New York: Knopf.

Elkind, D. (2001). Young Einsteins: Much too early. *Education Matters, 1*(2), 9–15.

El-Nemr, M. A. (1979). *Meta-analysis of the outcomes of teaching biology as inquiry*. Unpublished doctoral dissertation. Boulder: University of Colorado.

Gao, H. (2005, April 11). Kindergarten or "kindergrind"? School getting tougher for kids. *San Diego Union-Tribune.*

Glazerman, S., Dolfin, S., Bleeker, M., Johnson, A., Isenberg, E., Lugo-Gel, J., et al. (2009). *Impacts of comprehensive teacher induction: Results from the first year of a randomized control study.* Washington, DC: Institute of Educational Sciences, National Center for Education Evaluation and Regional Assistance, U.S. Department of Education.

Glickman, C. D. (1990). *Supervision of instruction: A developmental approach.* Boston: Allyn & Bacon.

Goldhammer, R., Anderson, R. H., & Krajewski, R. (1980). *Clinical supervision: Special methods for the supervision of teachers* (2nd ed.). New York: Holt, Rinehart, and Winston.

Gunning, T. (1998). *Best books for beginning readers.* Boston: Allyn & Bacon.

Hall, B. (2004). Literacy coaches: An evolving role. *Carnegie Newsletter, 3*(1). Available August 24, 2009, at http://www.carnegie.org/reporter/09/literacy/index.html

Hanson, R., & Farrell, D. (1995). The long-term effects on high school seniors of learning to read in kindergarten. *Reading Research Quarterly, 30*(4), 908–933.

Harkreader, S., & Weathersby, J. (1998). *Staff development and student achievement: Making the connection in Georgia's schools.* Atlanta: Council for School Performance, Georgia State University.

Harvey, O. J., Hunt, D., & Schroder, H. (1961). *Conceptual systems and personality organization.* New York: John Wiley and Sons.

Hillocks, G. (1987). Synthesis of research on teaching writing. *Educational Leadership, 44*(8), 71–82.

Hord, S. M., & Sommers, W. A. (2008). *Leading professional learning communities: Voices from research and practice.* Thousand Oaks: Corwin.

Huberman, A. M. (1992). Critical introduction. In M. Fullan, *Successful school improvement: The implementation perspective and beyond* (pp. 1–20). Philadelphia: Open University Press.

Huberman, A. M., & Miles, M. B. (1984). *Innovation up close: How school improvement works.* New York: Plenum.

Hunt, D. (1981). *Teachers' personal theorizing.* Toronto, Canada: Ontario Institute for Studies in Education.

Hunter, M. (1980). Six types of supervisory conferences. *Educational Leadership, 37,* 408–412.

International Reading Association (IRA). (1998). *Position statement on phonemic awareness and the teaching of reading.* Newark, DE: Author.

International Reading Association (IRA). (2004). Coaches, controversy, consensus. *Reading Today, 21*(5), 1.

International Reading Association (IRA) & National Association for the Education of Young Children (NAEYC). (1998). *Position statement on learning to read and write: Developmentally appropriate practices for young children.* Newark, DE: International Reading Association.

Iowa Association of School Boards. (2007). *Leadership for student learning* [book & DVD]. Des Moines, IA: Author.

James-Bardurny, S., Mansfield, W., Deke, J., Carey, N., Lugo-Gil, J., Hershey, A., Douglas, A., Gersten, R., Newman-Gonchar, R., Dimino, J., Faddis, B., &

Pendleton, A. (2009). *Effectiveness of selected supplemental reading comprehension interventions: Impacts on a first cohort of fifth-grade students* (2009-4032). Washington, DC: Institute of Educational Sciences, National Center for Education Evaluation and Regional Assistance, U.S. Department of Education.

Joyce, B., Brown, C. C., & Peck, L. (1981). *Flexibility in teaching: An excursion into the nature of teaching and training.* New York: Longman.

Joyce, B., Calhoun, E., Carran, N., Simser, J., Rust, D., & Halliburton, C. (1996). University Town Program: Exploring governance structures. In B. Joyce & E. Calhoun (Eds.), *Learning experiences in school renewal: An exploration of five successful programs* (pp. 52–93). Eugene, OR: ERIC Clearinghouse on Educational Management.

Joyce, B., Calhoun, E., & Hopkins, D. (1999). *The new structure of school improvement: Inquiring schools and achieving students.* Buckingham, England: Open University Press.

Joyce, B., Calhoun, E., & Hrycauk, M. (2001). A second chance for struggling readers. *Educational Leadership, 58*(6), 42–47.

Joyce, B., Calhoun, E., Jutras, J., & Newlove, K. (2006, November). *Scaling up: The results of a literacy curriculum implemented in an entire education authority of 53 schools.* A paper delivered to the Asian Pacific Educational Research Association, Hong Kong.

Joyce, B., & Showers, B. (2002). *Student achievement through staff development* (3rd ed.). Alexandria, VA: Association for Supervision and Curriculum Development.

Joyce, B., & Weil, M. (with Calhoun, E.). (2008). *Models of teaching* (8th ed.). Boston: Pearson Education.

Joyce, B., & Wolf, J. M. (1996). Readersville: Building a culture of readers and writers. In B. Joyce & E. Calhoun (Eds.), *Learning experiences in school renewal: An exploration of five successful programs* (pp. 95–115). Eugene, OR: ERIC Clearinghouse on Educational Management.

Kaplan, A. (1998). *The conduct of inquiry: Methodology for behavioral science.* San Francisco: Chandler. (Original work published 1964)

Loucks-Horsley, S., Stiles, K. E., Mundry, S., Love, N., & Hewson, P. W. (2010). *Designing professional development for teachers of science and mathematics* (3rd ed.). Thousand Oaks, CA, Corwin.

McGill-Franzen, A., Allington, R., Yokoi, I., & Brooks, G. (1999). Putting books in the room seems necessary but not sufficient. *Journal of Educational Research, 93*, 67–74.

Murphy, C. U., & Lick, D. W. (2005). *Whole-faculty study groups: Creating professional learning communities that target student learning* (3rd ed.). Thousand Oaks, CA: Corwin.

Myers, M. (1985). *The teacher-researcher.* Urbana, IL: The National Council of Teachers of English.

Natale, J. (2001). Early learners: Are full-day academic kindergartens too much, too soon? *American School Board Journal, 188*(3), 22–25.

National Assessment of Educational Progress (NAEP). (2004). *Reading highlights, 2003.* Washington, DC: National Center for Educational Statistics.

Oja, S. N., & Smulyan, L. (1989). *Collaborative action research.* London: Falmer Press.

Pinnell, G. S., Lyone, C. A., Deford, D., Bryk, A., & Seltzer, M. (1994). Comparing instructional models for the literacy education of high-risk first graders. *Reading Research Quarterly, 29*(1), 9–38.

Rogers, D., Haven-O'Donnell, R., Hebdon, S., & Ferrell, F. (1990, April). *Lessons on relating research, reflection, and reform from three researcher/practitioner projects.* Paper presented at the annual meeting of the American Educational Research Association, Boston.

Sagor, R. (1992). *How to conduct collaborative action research.* Alexandria, VA: Association of Supervision and Curriculum Development.

Schaefer, R. (1967). *The school as a center of inquiry.* New York: Harper and Row.

Schmoker, M. (2004, February).The tipping point: From feckless reform to substantive instructional improvement. *Phi Delta Kappan, 85*(6), 424–432.

Schmoker, M. (2006). *Results now: How we can achieve unprecedented improvements in teaching and learning.* Alexandria, VA: Association for Supervision and Curriculum Development.

Schmuck, R., & Runkel, P. (1985). *The handbook of organizational development in schools.* Palo Alto, CA: Mayfield Press.

Schwab, J. (1965). *Biological sciences curriculum study: Biology teachers' handbook.* New York: Wiley.

Seashore-Lewis, K., & Miles, M. (1990). *Improving the urban high school.* New York: Teachers College Press.

Simon, A., & Boyer, G. (1966). *Mirrors for behavior.* Philadelphia: Research for Better Schools.

Sirotnik, K. (1983). What you see is what you get: Consistency, persistence, and mediocrity in classrooms. *Harvard Education Review, 53*(1), 16–31.

Slavin, R. E., & Madden, N. (2001). *One million children: Success for all.* Thousand Oaks, CA: Corwin.

Slavin, R. E., Madden, N. A., Chambers, B., & Haxby, B. (2009). *2 million children: Success for all* (2nd ed.). Thousand Oaks, CA: Corwin.

Smith, T. M., & Ingersall, R. M. (2004). What are the effects of induction and mentoring on beginning teacher turnover? *American Educational Research Journal, 41*(3), 681–714.

Strickland, R. (1988). The teacher as researcher. *Language Arts, 65*(8), 754–764.

Swartz, S., & Klein, A. (1997). *Research in reading recovery.* Portsmouth, NH: Heinemann.

Sweeny, B. W. (2008). *Leading the teacher induction and mentoring program* (2nd ed.). Thousand Oaks, CA: Corwin.

Wei, R. C., Darling-Hammond, L., Andree, A., Richardson, N., & Orphanos, S. (2009). *Professional learning in the learning profession: A status report on teacher development in the United States and abroad; Technical report.* Dallas, TX: National Staff Development Council.

Wiederholt, J. L., & Bryant, B. (2001). *Gray oral reading tests.* Austin, TX: Pro-Ed.

Wolf, J. M. (1998). Just read. *Educational Leadership, 55*(8), 61–63.

Other Suggested Readings

Adey, P. (with Hewitt, G., Hewitt, J., & Landau, N.). (2004). *The professional development of teachers: Practice and theory.* Dordrecht, The Netherlands: Kluwer Academic.

Adger, C. T., Hoyle, S. M., & Dickinson, D. K. (2004). Locating learning in in-service education for preservice teachers. *American Educational Research Journal, 41*(4), 867–900.

Alkin, M. (Ed.). (1992). *Encyclopedia of educational research* (6th ed.). New York: Macmillan.

Allington, R. (Ed.). (2002). *Big brother and the national reading curriculum.* Portsmouth, NH: Heinemann.

American Institutes for Research. (1999). *Designing effective professional development: Lessons from the Eisenhower program, executive summary.* Washington, DC: American Institutes for Research.

Association for Supervision and Curriculum Development. (2009). *Professional development online.* Available August 24, 2009, at http://www .ascd.org/professional_development/PD_Online_Courses.aspx. If you enroll, you are eligible to receive graduate credit through Adams State College, Alamosa, CO.

Atkinson, M., French, D., & Hastings, M. (2002). *Building professional collaborative cultures.* Boston: Center for Collaborative Education.

Bartell, C. (2005). *Cultivating high-quality teaching through induction and mentoring.* Thousand Oaks, CA: Corwin.

Bereiter, C. (1984). Constructivism, socioculturalism, and Popper's World 3. *Educational Researcher, 23*(7), 21–23.

Bereiter, C. (1997). Situated cognition and how to overcome it. In D. Kirshner & W. Whitson (Eds.), *Situated cognition: Social, semiotic, and psychological perspectives* (pp. 281–300). Hillsdale, NJ: Erlbaum.

Berman, P., & Gjelten, T. (1983). *Improving school improvement.* Berkeley, CA: Berman, Weiler Associates.

Bonsangue, M. (1993). Long-term effects of the Calculus Workshop Model. *Cooperative Learning, 13*(3), 19–20.

Borman, G. D., Slavin, R. E., Cheung, A., Chamberlain, A. M., Madden, N. A., & Chambers, B. (2005). Success for all: First-year results from the National Randomized Field Trial. *Educational Evaluation and Policy Analysis, 27*(1), 1–22.

Braden, V., & Bruns, B. (1977). *Tennis for the future.* Boston: Little, Brown.

Bredderman, T. (1978). *Elementary school process curricula: A meta-analysis.* Albany: State University of New York.

Calhoun, E. (1997). *Literacy for all.* Saint Simons Island, GA: Phoenix Alliance.

Chin, R., & Benne, K. (1969). General strategies for effecting change in human systems. In W. Bennis, K. Benne, & R. Chin (Eds.), *The planning of change* (pp. 32–59). New york: Holt, Rinehart, and Winston.

Clark, C. (2007, January 11). [Review of the book *Studying teacher education: The report of the AERA Panel on Research and Teacher Education*]. *Teachers College Record.*

Cochran-Smith, M., & Zeichner, K. (2005). *Studying teacher education: The report of the AERA Panel on Research and Teacher Education.* Mahwah, NJ: Erlbaum.

Cook, C. J. (1997). *Critical issue: Finding time for professional development.* Available August 24, 2009, at North Central Regional Educational Laboratory Web site: http://www.ncrel.org/sdrs/areas/issues/educatrs/profdevl/pd300.htm

Cornelius-White, J., & Cornelius-White, C. (2005). Nondirective education. In B. Levitt (Ed.), *On being nondirective* (pp. 314–323). Ross-on-Wye, United Kingdom: PCCS Books.

Council of Chief State School Officers. (1996). *Professional development: Making a vision become reality in high-poverty schools.* Washington, DC: Author.

Cuban, L. (2003). *Oversold and underused: Computers in the classroom.* Cambridge, MA: Harvard University Press.

Cunningham, J. W. (2002). [Review of *The National Reading Panel report*]. In R. Allington (Ed.), *Big Brother and the National Reading Curriculum: How ideology trumped evidence* (pp. 49–74). Portsmouth, NH: Heinemann.

Cunningham, A. (2005). Vocabulary growth through independent reading and reading aloud to children. In E. Hiebert & M. Kamil (Eds.), *Teaching and learning vocabulary* (pp. 45–68). Mahwah, NJ: Erlbaum.

Daane, M., Campbell, J., Grigg, W., Goodman, M., & Oranje, A. (2005). *The nation's report card.* Washington, DC: National Center for Educational Statistics.

Darling-Hammond, L., Wei, R., Andree, A., Richardson, N., & Orphanos, S. (2009b). State of the profession. *Journal of Teacher Education, 30*(2), 42–50.

Dicker, M. (1990). Using action research to navigate an unfamiliar teaching assignment. *Theory into Practice, 29*(3), 203–208.

Duffy, G. G. (2003). *Explaining reading: A resource for teaching concepts, skills, and strategies.* New York: Guilford.

Education Alliance at Brown University. (2009). *Online professional development.* Available August 24, 2009, at http://www.alliance.brown.edu/ae_onlinelearn.php

Ehri, L., Nunes, S., Stahl, S., & Willows, D. (2001). Systematic phonics instruction helps students learn to read. *Review of Educational Research, 71*(3), 393–447.

Elmore, R. F. (2002). *Bridging the gap between standards and achievement.* New York: Albert Shanker Institute.

Elmore, R. F. (2004). *School reform from the inside out: Policy, practice, and performance.* Cambridge, MA: Harvard University Press.

Fenstermacher, G., & Richardson, V. (2005). *On making determinations of quality in teaching.* New York: Teachers College Record.

Flanders, N. (1970). *Analyzing teaching behavior.* Reading, MA: Addison-Wesley.

Fullan, M. (1999). *Change forces: The sequel.* Philadelphia: Palmer Press.

Fullan, M. (2005). *Leadership & sustainability: System thinkers in action.* Thousand Oaks, CA: Corwin.

Fullan, M. (2006). *Breakthrough.* Thousand Oaks, CA: Corwin.

Garan, E. (2002). Beyond the smoke and mirrors: A critique of the National Reading Panel report on phonics. In R. Allington (Ed.), *Big brother and the national reading curriculum* (pp. 90–111). Portsmouth, NH: Heinemann.

Garan, E. (2005). Murder your darlings: A scientific response to the voice of evidence in reading research. *Phi Delta Kappan, 86*(6), 438–443.

Gentzler, Y. (2005). *A new teacher's guide to best practices.* Thousand Oaks, CA: Corwin.

Global Equine Academy. (2004). *An equine college that is affordable.* Sundance, WY: Author.

Grey, C., & Bishop, Q. (2009). Leadership development. *Journal of Staff Development, 30*(1), 28–33.

Guskey, T. (1994). Results-oriented professional development: In search of an optimal mix of effective practices. *Journal of Staff Development, 15*(4), 42–50.

Harvard University Graduate School of Education. (2009). *Professional education.* Available August 24, 2009, at the Harvard University Web site: http://gseweb.harvard.edu/profed/index.html. Offers on-site and online professional development.

Hill, H., Rowan, B., & Ball, D. (2005). Effects of teachers' mathematical knowledge on student achievement. *American Educational Research Journal, 42*(2), 371–406.

Hopkins, D. (1985). *A teacher's guide to educational research.* Philadelphia: Open University Press.

Hord, S. M. (2009). Professional learning communities. *Journal of Staff Development, 30*(1), 40–43.

Horsley, S. (1990). *Elementary school science for the 90s.* Alexandria, VA: Association for Supervision and Curriculum Development.

Hunt, D. (1981). *Teachers' personal theorizing.* Toronto, Canada: Ontario Institute for Studies in Education.

Husby, V. (2005). *Individualizing professional development.* Thousand Oaks, CA: Corwin.

International Reading Association (IRA). (2006). *Standards for middle school and high school literacy coaches.* Newark, DE: Author.

Iowa Association of School Boards. (2000). *The lighthouse study.* Des Moines, IA: Author.

Iowa Association of School Boards. (2007). *Leadership for student learning* [book & DVD]. Des Moines, IA: Author.

Jason, M. (2008). *Evaluating programs to increase student achievement.* Glenview, IL: Skylight/Pearson.

Johnson, D., Johnson, R., & Stanne, M. B. (2000). *Cooperative learning methods: A meta-analysis.* Minneapolis: University of Minnesota.

Joyce, B. (1999). Reading about reading: Notes from a consumer to the scholars of literacy. *Reading Teacher, 52*(7), 662–671.

Joyce, B. (2004). How are professional learning communities created? History has a few messages. *Phi Delta Kappan, 86*(1), 76–83.

Joyce, B., & Belitzky, A. (2000). *Developing a human resource system for educators.* Tallahassee: Florida State Department of Education.

Joyce, B., Calhoun, E., & Hrycauk, M. (2003). Learning to read in kindergarten. *Phi Delta Kappan, 85*(2), 126–132.

Joyce, B., Calhoun, E., Hrycauk, M., & Hrycauk. (2006, November). *The tending of diversity through a robust core literacy curriculum: Gender, socioeconomic status, learning disabilities, and ethnicity.* A paper delivered to the Asian Pacific Educational Research Association, Hong Kong.

Joyce, B., & Harootunian, B. (1970). *The structure of teaching.* Chicago: Science Research Associates.

Joyce, B., Hrycauk, M., Calhoun, E., & Hrycauk, W. (2006, November). *The tending of diversity through a robust core literacy curriculum: Gender, socioeconomic status, learning disabilities, and ethnicity.* A paper delivered to the Asian Pacific Educational Research Association, Hong Kong.

Joyce, B., Weil, M., Wald, R., Gullion, C., Feller, M., & McKibbin, M. (1972). *Models of teaching as a paradigm for teaching education.* New York: Teachers College, Columbia University. (ERIC Document Reproduction Service No. ED062301). In this fall 1970 study, student teachers were exposed to three models of teaching, and teacher behavior and student response were coded using the Teacher Innovator System (TIS).

Keeley, P. (2005). *Science curriculum topic study: Bridging the gap between standards and practice.* Thousand Oaks, CA: Corwin.

Keller, B. (2008). Teacher coaches find a growing role. *Teacher Magazine, 1*(2), 4, 6.

Kise, J. A. G. (2006). *Differentiated coaching: A framework for helping teachers change.* Thousand Oaks, CA: Corwin.

Kise, J. A. G., & Russell, B. (2008). *Differentiated school leadership: Effective collaboration, communication, and change through personality type.* Thousand Oaks, CA: Corwin.

Knight, J. (2007). *Instructional coaching: A partnership approach to improving instruction.* Thousand Oaks, CA: Corwin.

Krashen, S. (2005). Is in-school free reading good for children? Why the National Reading Panel Report is (still) wrong. *Phi Delta Kappan, 85*(6), 444–447.

Kuhn, T. (1962). *The structure of scientific revolutions.* Chicago: The University of Chicago Press.

Leonard, H. A., Winkler, J. D., Hove, A., Ettedgui, E., Shanley, M. G., & Sollinger, J. (2001). *Enhancing stability and professional development using distance learning* (MR-1317-A). Santa Monica, CA: RAND. Available August 24, 2009, at http://www.rand.org/pubs/monograph_reports/MR1317/index.html

Lieberman, A., & Miller, L. (1992). Professional development of teachers. In M. C. Alkin (Ed.), *Encyclopedia of educational research* (6th ed., pp. 1045–1051). New York: The Free Press.

Literacy coach confidential: Teachers resent me—what can I do? (n.d.) Available August 24, 2009, at http://www.choiceliteracy.com/public/104.cfm

Lyons, C., & Pinnell, G. (2001). *Systems for change in literacy education: A guide to professional development.* Portsmouth, NH: Heinemann.

Manzo, K. (2005a, June 22). Complaint filed against reading initiative. *Education Week.*

Manzo, K. (2005b, October 12). GAO to probe federal plan for reading. *Education Week.*

Manzo, K. (2005c, September 8). States pressed to refashion Reading First grant designs. *Education Week.*

Marick. R. (1990). Seattle portable writing project. *Teacher Leadership.* Seattle, WA: Puget Sound Educational Consortium.

Marzano, R. (2003). *What works in schools.* Alexandria, VA: Association for Supervision and Curriculum Development.

McGill-Franzen, A., & Allington, R. L. (1991). Every child's right: Literacy. *Reading Teacher, 45,* 86–90.

McGill-Franzen, A., & Goatley, V. (2001). Title I and special education: Support for children who struggle to learn to read. In S. Neuman & D. Dickinson (Eds.), *Handbook of early literacy research* (pp. 471–483). New York: Guilford Press.

Miles, M., & Huberman, A. (1984). *Qualitative data analysis.* Beverly Hills, CA: Sage.

Mitchell, D., & Scott-Hendrick, L. (2007). *California beginning teacher support and assessment and intern alternative certification evaluation study.* Riverside: University of California—Riverside.

Muncey, D., & McQuillan, P. (1993). Preliminary findings from a five-year study of the Coalition of Essential Schools. *Phi Delta Kappan, 74*(6), 486–489.

Nagy, W., & Anderson, P. (1987). Breadth and depth in vocabulary knowledge. *Reading Research Quarterly, 19,* 304–330.

Natale, J. (2001). Early learners: Are full-day academic kindergartens too much, too soon? *American School Board Journal, 188*(3), 22–25.

National Center for Educational Statistics (NCES). (1998). Long-term trends in reading performance. *NAEP Facts, 3*(1). Available August 24, 2009, at http://nces.ed.gov/pubs98/98464.pdf

National Reading Panel. (2000). *Teaching children to read: An evidence-based assessment of the scientific research literature on reading and its implications for reading instruction.* Rockville, MD: National Institute of Child Health and Human Development.

National Staff Development Council (NSDC). (2004a). [Advertisement in the *Phi Delta Kappan*]. *Phi Delta Kappan, 86*(3), 187.

National Staff Development Council (NSDC). (2004b). [Advertisement in the *Phi Delta Kappan.*] *Phi Delta Kappan, 86*(4), inside cover.

National Staff Development Council (NSDC) and National Institute for Community Innovations (NICI) (2001). *E-learning for educators: Implementing the standards for staff development.* Oxford, OH: National Staff Development Council. Available August 24, 2009, at http://www.nsdc.org/news/authors/e-learning.pdf

Office of Manpower Economics. (2008). *The teachers' workload survey.* London: Author.

Oja, S. N., & Smulyan, L. (1989). *Collaborative action research.* London: Falmer Press.

Organization for Economic Cooperation and Development (OECD). (2007). *Education at a glance 2007.* Paris: Author.

Pardini, P. (1999). Making time for adult learning. *Journal of Staff Development, 20*(2), 37–41.

PBS Teacherline. (2005). *An introduction to underlying principles and research for effective literacy instruction.* Washington, DC: PBS Electronic Catalog.

Phillips, D. C. (1983). After the wake: Postpositivistic educational thought. *Educational Researcher, 12*(5), 4–12.

Phillips, D. C. (1995). The good, the bad, and the ugly: The many faces of constructivism. *Educational Researcher, 24*(7), 5–12.

Pinnell, G. S. (1989). Helping at-risk children learn to read. *Elementary School Journal, 90*(2), 161–184.

Popper, K. (2002). *The logic of scientific discovery* (New ed.). London: Routledge. (Original work published as *Logik der Forschung* in 1935)

Pressley, M., & Woloshyn, V. (Eds.). (1995). *Cognitive strategy instruction that really improves children's academic performance* (2nd ed.). Cambridge, MA: Brookline.

Rice, D., Delagardelle, M., Buckton, M., Jons, C., Lueders, W., Vens, M. J., Joyce, B., Wolf, J., & Weathersby, J. (2001, April). *The lighthouse inquiry: School board/superintendent behaviors in school districts with extreme differences in student achievement.* Paper presented to the annual meeting of the American Educational Research Association, Seattle, WA. (ERIC Document Reproduction Service No. ED453172)

Richardson, J. (2008). A fresh perspective. *The learning system, 3*(6), 1, 6.

Richardson, V., & Placier, P. (2001). Teacher change. In V. Richardson (Ed.), *Handbook of research on teaching* (4th ed., pp. 905–950). Washington, DC: American Educational Research Association.

Robbins, P. (1991). *How to plan and implement a peer coaching program.* Alexandria, VA: Association for Supervision and Curriculum Development.

Sanders, W. R., & Burnside, B. L. (2001). *Assessment of initial delivery of the Armor Captains Career Course (distance learning)* (Research Report 1775). Alexandria, VA: U.S. Army Research Institute for the Behavioral and Social Sciences. Available August 24, 2009, at http://www.hqda.army .mil/ari/pdf/RR1775.pdf. General evaluation of sections of the course delivered by distance means. See also Army Distributed Learning Program Web site: http://www.tradoc.army.mil/tadlp/

Scherer, M. (2005). Perspectives. *Educational Leadership, 82*(8), 7.

Schmoker, M. (2001, October 24). The "Crayola curriculum." *Education Week,* 42–44.

Schwab, J. (1982). *Science, curriculum, and liberal education.* Chicago: University of Chicago Press.

Showers, B., Joyce, B., Scanlon, M., & Schnaubelt, C. (1998). A second chance to learn to read. *Educational Leadership, 55*(6), 27–31.

Silin, J., & Schwartz, F. (2003). Staying close to the teacher. *Teachers College Record Journal, 41*(3), 681–714.

Slavin, R. E., Madden, N. A., Dolan, L., & Wasik, B. (1996). *Every child, every school: Success for all.* Thousand Oaks, CA: Corwin.

Slavin, R. E., Madden, N. A., Karweit, N., Dolan, L., & Wasik, B. (1990). *Success for all: Effects of variations in duration and resources of a statewide elementary restructuring program* (CDS Report No. 2). Baltimore, MD: Center for Research on Effective Schooling for Disadvantaged Students, Johns Hopkins University.

Snow, C., Burns, M., & Griffin, P. (1998). *Preventing reading difficulties in young children.* Washington, DC: National Academy Press.

Sparks, D. (2001). *E-learning for educators: Implementing the standards for staff development.* Oxford, OH: National Staff Development Council.

Sparks, D., & Hirsh, S. (1997). *A new vision for staff development.* Alexandria, VA: Association for Supervision and Staff Development.

Speck, M., & Knipe, C. (2005). *Why can't we get it right? Designing high-quality professional development for standards-based schools.* Thousand Oaks, CA: Corwin.

Stauffer, R. (1969). *Directing reading maturity as a cognitive-learning process.* New York: Harper and Row.

Stauffer, R. (1970). *The language-experience approach to the teaching of reading.* New York: Harper and Row.

Stepanek, J., Appel, G, Leong, M., Mangan, M. T., & Mitchell, M. (2007). *Leading lesson study: A practical guide for teachers and facilitators.* Thousand Oaks, CA: Corwin.

Stevenson, H. W. (1998). Guarding teachers' time. *Education Week, 18*(2), 52.

Toppo, G. (2005a, August 8). Federally funded Reading First called into question. *USA Today.*

Toppo, G. (2005b, October 10). Reading program raises questions for lawmakers. *USA Today.*

Vance, V., & Schlecty, P. (1982). The distribution of academic ability in the teaching force: Policy implications. *Phi Delta Kappan, 64*(1), 22–27.

Villani, S. (2009). *Comprehensive mentoring programs for new teachers: Models of induction and support* (2nd ed.). Thousand Oaks, CA: Corwin.

Walston, J., & West, J. (2004). *Full-day and half-day kindergarten in the United States: Findings from the early childhood longitudinal study, kindergarten class of 1998–99* (NCES 2004-078). Washington, DC: U.S. Department of Education, National Center for Education Statistics.

Wiebke, K., & Bardin, J. (2009). New teacher support. *Journal of Staff Development, 30*(1), 34–39.

Wilmore, E. (2007). *Teacher leadership: Improving teaching and learning from inside the classroom.* Thousand Oaks, CA: Corwin.

Wilson, S., & Berne, J. (1999). Teacher learning and the acquisition of professional knowledge: An examination of research on contemporary professional development. In A. Iran-Nejad & P. D. Pearson (Eds.), *Review of research in education* (Vol. 24, pp. 173–209). Washington, DC: American Educational Research Association.

Wood, K. D., & Tinajero, J. (2002). Using pictures to teach content to second language learners. *Middle School Journal, 33*(5), 47–51.

Xue, Y., & Meisels, S. (2004). Early literacy instruction and learning in kindergarten. *American Educational Research Journal, 41*(1), 191–229.

Yoon, K., Duncan, T., Lee, S. W.-Y., Scarloss, B., & Shapley, K. (2007). *Reviewing the evidence on how teacher professional development affects student achievement.* Washington, DC: U.S. Department of Education.

Index

Acknowledgments

We have enjoyed writing this book. We owe a lot of people for that enjoyment and the professional satisfaction that comes with it.

Several thousand of these people are the teachers who have allowed us to study them, study with them, and try to help them build their professional competence.

Several hundred books, articles, and monographs have fed us, and we especially owe those who have developed and tested their ideas. Joe Schwab, Shlomo Sharon, Robert Schaefer, Frances Fuller, Walter Borg, John Goodlad, and Carl Glickman represent them.

School improvement programs have provided the settings for much of our most important experience and the opportunity to conduct formal studies. Our colleagues/collaborators in those districts are serious family. Members include Carlene Murphy in Augusta, Georgia; Nina Carran in Ames, Iowa; Jan Fisher and Jackie Wiseman in Newport, California; Marilyn Hrycauk, Walter Hrycauk, and Lisa Mueller in the Northern Lights schools in Bonnyville, Alberta, Canada; and Jim Jutras, Kim Newlove, and Lori and Ralph Kindrachuk in Saskatoon, Saskatchewan, Canada.

Others have been the lead investigators in studies where one or the other of us was on the team: David Hunt, Jeanie Posey, Mary Delagardelle, and Beverly Showers. We have been fortunate to have considerable experience in both Europe and Asia, where we have learned how much we have in common with educational practice in other nations and cultures. In the United Kingdom we have worked and authored with David Hopkins and are indebted to Shona Mullen and the editors at the Open University Press.

Routines can cause vapidity—a loss of meaning. Custom has especially staled the meaning of authors' kudos to the folks in the publisher's house. We have had wonderful support, first from Dan Alpert and then from Paula Fleming. Never has it been more or better as we have, between us, birthed over 30 books and monographs.

Additionally, Corwin would like to thank Dixie Keyes, Assistant Professor at Arkansas State University and Director of the Arkansas Delta Writing Project, along with Jim Jutras, Director of Education at Saskatoon Public Schools, for serving as peer reviewers.

About the Authors

Bruce Joyce grew up in New Jersey, was educated at Brown University, and, after military service, taught in the schools of Delaware. He was a professor at the University of Delaware; the University of Chicago; and Teachers College, Columbia University, where he directed the laboratory school and the elementary teacher education program.

His research and writing are focused on models of teaching and professional development and the social studies.

He lives in Saint Simons Island, Georgia.

Emily Calhoun currently focuses on school improvement and professional development, where she combines practice and research. She specializes in the language arts, particularly the teaching of reading and writing in the primary grades and programs for struggling readers K–12. She grew up in Georgia and was educated there, including Georgia College, Southeastern Georgia College, and the University of Georgia, where she received her doctorate.

Her writing includes books on action research, the Picture Word Inductive Model of Teaching, assessing reading programs, and models of teaching.

She lives in Saint Simons Island, Georgia.

Booksend Laboratories DVDs

A series of DVDs are available on topics relevant to models of professional development. Some are discussions and presentations by Bruce Joyce and Emily Calhoun. Others are demonstrations of curricular and instructional models described in the book. To discuss and order, call 912-634-4759.

CORWIN
A SAGE Company

The Corwin logo—a raven striding across an open book—represents the union of courage and learning. Corwin is committed to improving education for all learners by publishing books and other professional development resources for those serving the field of PreK–12 education. By providing practical, hands-on materials, Corwin continues to carry out the promise of its motto: **"Helping Educators Do Their Work Better."**

NSDC's purpose: Every educator engages in effective professional learning every day so every student achieves.